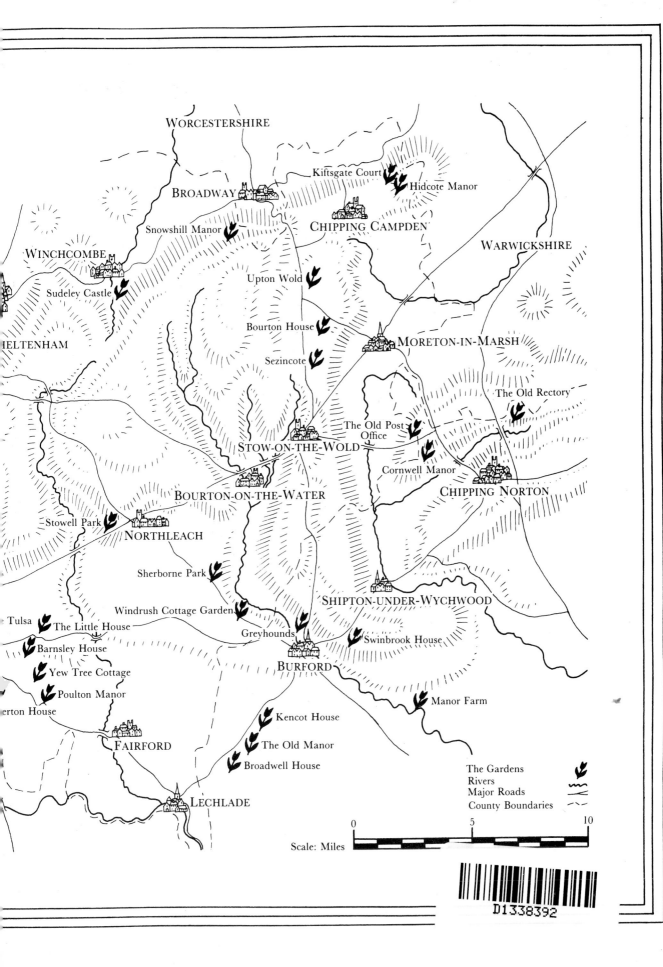

WORCESTERSHIRE

BROADWAY

Kiftsgate Court

Hidcote Manor

Snowshill Manor

CHIPPING CAMPDEN

WARWICKSHIRE

WINCHCOMBE

Upton Wold

Sudeley Castle

Bourton House

IELTENHAM

Sezincote

MORETON-IN-MARSH

The Old Rectory

The Old Post
Office

STOW-ON-THE-WOLD

BOURTON-ON-THE-WATER

Cornwell Manor

CHIPPING NORTON

Stowell Park

NORTHLEACH

Sherborne Park

SHIPTON-UNDER-WYCHWOOD

Windrush Cottage Garden

Tulsa

The Little House

Greyhounds

Swinbrook House

Barnsley House

Yew Tree Cottage

BURFORD

Poulton Manor

Manor Farm

erton House

Kencot House

FAIRFORD

The Old Manor

Broadwell House

LECHLADE

The Gardens
Rivers
Major Roads
County Boundaries

0   5   10

Scale: Miles

D1338392

OVER THE HILLS FROM BROADWAY

This book is dedicated by David Wheeler
to his mother, Lily, and to the memory
of his father, Arthur

and by Simon Dorrell
to his parents, Jean and Jim

OVER THE HILLS FROM BROADWAY

Images of Cotswold Gardens

by
David Wheeler
with paintings and drawings by
Simon Dorrell

Foreword by Rosemary Verey

ALAN SUTTON

First published in the United Kingdom in 1991
Alan Sutton Publishing Ltd · Phoenix Mill · Far Thrupp · Stroud · Gloucestershire

British Library Cataloguing in Publication Data

Wheeler, David *1945–*
Over the hills from Broadway: images of Cotswold gardens.
1. England, Paintings, Special subjects, gardens
I. Title II. Dorrell, Simon *1961–*
758.5

ISBN 0–86299–793–3

Typeset in 11/13 Baskerville.
Typesetting and origination by
Alan Sutton Publishing Limited.
Colour separation by
Yeo Valley Reprographics, Wells.
Printed in Great Britain by
Eagle Colour Books, Glasgow.

CONTENTS

FOREWORD

David Wheeler and Simon Dorrell, who live in Wales, have
travelled over the hills from Broadway to record their vivid and
fresh impressions of Cotswold gardens. I have lived in the Cotswolds
for more than half a century: the beauty of our villages has been
impressed on my mind over these years, and I know that our Cotswold
gardens, with their alkaline soil, have a timeless yet contemporary
appeal, making them stand out unquestionably among the best
gardens of England. When friends commiserate with me that we
cannot grow azaleas, my spirit rejoices, knowing that clematis,
viburnums, sorbus and a host of other plants will prosper luxuriantly
here.

But Cotswold gardens are more than this. They have a tradition,
of formal as well as informal design, unique to themselves and
blending into the surrounding countryside. I am proud to live in the
Cotswolds. Colder they may be than Kent, less dramatic than
Northumberland, less temperate than Cornwall, but they have kept
their beauty through the ages and today are outstanding in their
diversity and appeal.

David Wheeler has discovered the beauty of these gardens, coming
on them with fresh eyes. He describes his selected gardens with a
clear and sensitive vision; without 'taking you round' each garden, he
nevertheless gives you the complete picture, with an intimate insight
and often from an unusual viewpoint. Today, gardening books are
illustrated with outstanding colour photographs, but the pages of this

book are imaginatively brought to life by Simon Dorrell's minutely detailed drawings and impressionistic colour paintings, reflecting and enhancing David Wheeler's words. Simon has caught the ghosts of Sudeley, the lovingly cared-for plants at Little Tulsa, the architecture of Newark Park and the Rococo garden at Painswick, the topiary at Rodmarton and Cornwell Manor and the drama of clipped evergreens at Broadwell, Mamie Gibbs's flair for planting at Ewen Manor, vegetables and violas at April Cottage and the idyllic riverside setting of Manor Farm among the ruins of Minster Lovell, the colour of the Cotswold stone and the atmosphere of the village street. What a breathtaking collection of images on which to dwell.

The Cotswolds have for centuries been a privileged place in which to live – privileged because of the beauty of the wolds and their contrasting valleys. The mellow stone and intimate character of the villages have beckoned to artists and craftsmen as well as to country-loving people, encouraging them to settle and work here and to create things of beauty and practise country crafts. Indeed, the title of this book is adapted from the first American guidebook to the Cotswolds, published in Philadelphia in the 1890s. Henry James had introduced the region to Americans in an article in *Harper's* in 1889 when describing the newly established artistic coterie that had settled around Broadway.

The Cotswold limestone plateau starts on top of the great cliff which spreads in an almost unbroken line from Dyrham to Dover's Hill near Chipping Campden and Broadway, then dips gently to the east and south-east to merge finally with the clay plains of Oxfordshire. This oolitic limestone has always provided fine-grained stone, easy to cut and carve when freshly quarried but hardening as it is exposed to the elements. It is a fine material for house building, the colours of the stone ranging from cream through shades of pale and rich yellow to deep brown, and as you drive through the Cotswolds you will notice these subtle variations. It provided stone tiles for roofing in Roman and medieval times, and occasionally also today. Then there are the fossils which helped to create the ragged slabs of ragstone, used by medieval shepherds to enclose their enormous sheep runs, and ever since for the dry stone walls so characteristic of the Cotswolds.

Fine houses and picturesque cottages have been built of this wonderful stone in every period, and gardens grand and small have been quick to grow up around them. Stone is also vital in these gardens, for walls and terraces, steps and paving, troughs and seats. One of the oldest secular buildings still serving as a family home is Beverston Castle, built before 1225 but much altered through fire. Its garden retains an atmosphere of antiquity with a moat and fine old trees. Later centuries have added their contributions, from the eighteenth-century gazebo to the present owner's generous planting of shrubs, old roses and specimen trees.

Newark Park, built as a hunting lodge in the mid-sixteenth century, stands precariously on the edge of the Cotswold escarpment. This beautiful house and its woodland garden were rescued by an American enthusiast, Robert Parsons, from a state of dereliction. Now snowdrops and cyclamen in masses stud the grass under old trees, terraces and woodland paths lead you to a lake below – it is a garden full of atmosphere, where many dramas and romances must surely have taken place in the past, and now it is almost transfixed in time – it is free-wheeling, enjoying the present as much as the past.

The Painswick Rococo Garden is enjoying a renaissance: Lord and Lady Dickinson are faithfully and passionately restoring the garden and its unique buildings as they were depicted by Thomas Robins in 1748. At Stancombe Park the garden has two parts, and now the folly garden with its lakes created around 1820 is once more an important element. This and the more formal garden round the house are a remarkable tribute to Gerda and Basil Barlow's energy and inspiration.

Names of famous people who have lived in these houses or have left their mark on the gardens crop up on almost every page of this book. Badminton House is famous for its parkland laid out around 1700 by George London, partner in Brompton Nursery with the royal gardener Henry Wise. George London worked at Badminton for the first Duchess of Beaufort, an ardent gardener; she had extensive parterres around the house and a conservatory of exotic plants. William Kent altered the park layout and built Worcester Lodge, creating the three-mile-long vista from the lodge to the house. Caroline, the present Duchess, is an equally enthusiastic and successful gardener –

it is good to know that the Badminton grounds are once more being given the love and care that befit the grandeur of the house.

Sezincote, one of my favourite gardens, is among the most interesting in the Cotswolds. Humphry Repton was consulted about the park. Thomas Daniell, the Indian topographical artist, made the design for the Indian bridge which carries the drive over a delightfully landscaped small valley. The planting along the stream side has been carried out on the advice of Graham Stuart Thomas. Sezincote, lovely at all seasons, is a garden to be visited several times in the year to discover its full beauty and charm.

Sir Edwin Lutyens designed a new wing to Misarden Park, the Elizabethan mansion with a spectacular situation overlooking steep wooded valleys. Gertrude Jekyll left her mark at Combend Manor, Elkestone, a house with later additions by Sidney Barnsley. She designed the garden late in her life without visiting the site; it is especially famous for the long herbaceous borders, with their careful colour schemes, grey and white giving way to pale, then stronger yellows, and orange, blues and reds, now replanted from her original plans.

Ernest and Sidney Barnsley were working in Gloucestershire at this time. The Barnsley brothers lived for a while at Pinbury Park with Ernest Gimson and their wives, making impressive plasterwork ceilings and stone fireplaces. All three were designers, influenced by William Morris, Norman Shaw, John Seddings and other pioneers of the high Victorian Arts and Crafts movement. Ernest Barnsley is the most important of the three for this book, for between 1910 and 1919 he was working as the architect of Rodmarton Manor and, with Mrs Claud Biddulph and her head gardener William Scrubey, as the designer of the garden, now a fascinating and living period piece. Since 1954 Mary Biddulph has cared for Rodmarton; she has carried on its traditional design and spirit and left her personal touch with the introduction of many rare and interesting plants.

In 1919 the architect Charles Paget Wade bought Snowshill Manor, now belonging to the National Trust. Together he and fellow architect Hugh Baillie Scott transformed the garden, using low walls, terraces and different levels to create gardens within the garden – much in the fashion of nearby Hidcote Manor. Visitors flock to the Cotswolds to see the garden at Hidcote. Lawrence Johnston started to conceive and create the garden in 1907, and before he died he handed it over to the National Trust. Little did he know how influential a part he was to play in English garden style this century – many of us have turned to Hidcote to learn and be inspired.

In this Cotswold circle there are present-day gardeners of national renown. Keith Steadman is a tree lover, an expert on willows, who allows climbers to envelope his house and shrubs to stretch and scramble. His garden is essentially one for those who appreciate controlled abandon. When I visit Westend House I never cease to be amazed and delighted at the luxuriance and imagination of Keith's planting.

Alvilde Lees-Milne's gardening philosophy is quite different from Keith Steadman's. She is an expert plantswoman – her garden is as full of plants as she is of imagination – but they must be disciplined, with box well clipped, standard roses conforming and colours all in harmony. Gardens reflect their owners' character, and Essex House garden is immaculate, successful.

It is not often that three generations of lady gardeners have such flair and horticultural skill as the owners of Kiftsgate Court. Heather Muir, helped by her neighbour Lawrence Johnston, first brought this garden to life. Since 1954 her daughter Diany Binny has made it famous, and now her own daughter, Anne Chambers, has taken on the role of guardian with knowledge and enthusiasm.

New gardens are being made by new owners. At Upton Wold, near Moreton-in-Marsh, Hal Moggridge is advising Caroline Bond on the garden originally designed by Brenda Colvin twelve years ago. This is a garden which will surely flower and flourish through the 1990s. So will the very personal small gardens planted by their owners. Penelope Mortimer's garden at The Old Post Office in Chastleton reflects her character – bold, sensitive, observant and essentially individualistic. These gardens, now occupied by a mix of country people and retired and young professionals, are influenced by their owners' artistry and embody a vital aspect of village life. Once upon a time the head gardener at the big house would bring home cuttings from his master's garden; today they may find their way there as presents but more likely as purchases from the local garden centre.

I am delighted that such a dedicated gardener as Prince Charles, who enjoys many aspects of country life, alert to present-day conservation and at the same time striding into the future, has agreed to be included in this book – without Highgrove a book on Cotswold gardens would be incomplete. The house is eighteenth-century, but the garden is now becoming essentially twentieth-century. Here the Princess of Wales can relax and Prince Charles continue to plan and dig – private moments bringing a refreshment of spirit for both amidst their public lives. So to all of us our gardens can be a source of happiness, healing and inspiration.

ROSEMARY VEREY
May 1991

INTRODUCTION

My first intake of air was Cotswold air, during an early October night whose frost, according to my mother, put paid to the beans for that year. My earliest childhood memory emanates from a garden – a Cotswold garden. I was born in a small house in the Golden Valley near Stroud, with views across to Minchinhampton Common and within shouting distance of the site where the first lawn-mower was made (in 1830) – now, coincidentally, occupied by the publishers of this book.

My father was a passionate amateur gardener, bringing form and army order to an undulating hillside. His regimented rows of vegetables kept a growing post-war family well fed, and while any little time or money left over may have been spent on a few ornamental plants, I suspect these were most likely scrounged or the outcome of swaps among friends and neighbours. Alas, my father died while still a young man, depriving me of an opportunity to quiz him about the acquisition of his stock.

Pride of place in our garden was an apple tree, 'Ellison's Orange', won by my father in the local council's garden competition in the early 1950s. I wonder if it flourishes still? Certainly my brother and I watched it eagerly to report on its first fruiting, but I doubt if we ever allowed the young apples to ripen fully; boys in those days could exchange them at school for colourful marbles.

I can remember, too, the plant which seemed to a child's eye to dominate the garden and the several limestone boulders near the front gate. We called it snow-on-the-mount, better known as snow-in-summer, and if I was ever told its Latin name, *Cerastium tomentosum*, I would no doubt have thought it unnecessarily dull or plain pointless. But snow-on-the-mount was picked by my friends and me by the handsful in summer holidays along with jam-jarsful of rose petals for our own crude version of scent which, disappointingly, always turned out no more exciting than vaguely perfumed washing-up water with much the same complexion. I was encouraged to sow my own patch of flower seeds, and I can remember thinking then how puny and dreary the little flecks inside the bright packets seemed: would this *dust* lie in the ground and then suddenly burst into jolly rows of colourful blooms?

In springtime my brother and I would pick armsful of the cowslips and bluebells which profusely scattered the countryside – but that is a risky admission in these conservation-minded days. I was pleased to see, though, that our secret gathering places, tucked away in wooded clearings, seemed just as flowery in 1990.

I spent the first ten years of my life in the Cotswolds, and while I knew the countryside and country ways as a boy does, I was quite ignorant of the magnificent gardens which surrounded us. There was no car in the family and our furthest outings were afternoon meanderings across the fields to Sunday School at Brimscombe, evening walks *en famille* to Minchinhampton Common, or magical journeys to Stroud on the railcar which ran beside the canal past dangerously deep locks festooned with bright yellow water-lilies and boy-high reeds. I was ignorant of the Cotswold Arts and Crafts tradition and of the dedicated men whose hammers and anvils must earlier have reverberated through the broadleaf valleys as the craftsmen dressed their pieces of stone and fashioned ironwork for garden walls and gates. Ernest Gimson, the Barnsley brothers and Norman Jewson – names forever linked with twentieth-century Cotswold houses and gardens – all lived and worked for important parts of their lives at nearby Sapperton.

In his book, *By Chance I Did Rove* – privately published in 1951 and reissued by Rosemary Verey's daughter (Diana Wynne-Jones, Gryffon Publications) in 1986 – Norman Jewson remarks upon the wild flowers he saw as he went about the country lanes. There were periwinkle, deep crimson bloody cranesbill and pink-flowered wood sorrel. As part of Jewson's training, Ernest Gimson suggested that he should bring a different flower to the workshop each day to draw. I have no doubt that this could be achieved then; and perhaps again, now, as local authorities seem to have abandoned their disgraceful practice of spraying the roadsides with ruthless herbicides.

Throughout our days visiting gardens for this book between Easter and October 1990 we, too, marvelled at the verge-side wildlings still to be observed in great quantity. They included the eminently garden-worthy meadow cranesbill, *Geranium pratense*, whose delicate petals so closely resemble the colour of Chalk Blue butterflies. Norman Jewson also mentions pennywort, toadflax, pellitory and stonecrop growing on the drystone walls, and snake's-head fritillaries at Oaksey, pasque flowers near the Fosse Way and wild daffodils at Battlescombe. Anyone today who has travelled through the Cotswolds in the late winter months will have noticed snowdrops and primroses which at times can be so bountiful as to be a distraction to drivers. (Is it a coincidence, I wonder, that two men whose names are associated with snowdrops – James Atkins, 1804–1884, in *Galanthus nivalis* 'Atkinsii', and Henry Elwes, 1846–1922, in *G. elwesii* – either lived or were born in the Cotswolds?)

This galaxy of naturally-occurring flowers makes it possible to realise what a small step it is to assembling a wonderful collection of plants in a garden, and it would be possible, I am sure, to have an interesting Cotswold garden composed only of those native wild flowers endemic to the limestone regions of Britain.

I now live in Wales, my father's homeland. (Did he, I wonder, gaze wistfully across the Severn to the Welsh mountains on those Sunday evenings on Minchinhampton Common?) My life now revolves professionally around gardens; I edit the gardening journal HORTUS which I founded in 1987 and Simon Dorrell, whose paintings and drawings are presented in this book, is its art editor. Our combined interest in gardens and plants led to this collaboration, which we at least have found to be a delightful undertaking. Simon's youth was spent near Bewdley in Worcestershire, a county which can claim a small proportion of Cotswold territory near its southern boundary. One of his 'playground' haunts as a child was Sandbourne, where Gertrude Jekyll planned the garden, long since sunk beneath a housing estate. In his college days in Kent he frequented the garden at Sissinghurst Castle, where he was inspired to produce a series of paintings. Since coming to live in Wales he has prepared and exhibited a collection of pictures revealing some of the beauty to be found in the almost unknown gardens along the Welsh borders.

Why have we chosen to put together a book illustrated with paintings and drawings, rather than photographs? Our subtitle for this book contains the word 'images', and it is on the basis of this somewhat imprecise word that we have approached our subject. Photography, colour as well as black and white, has reached high levels of proficiency nowadays, and in many cases printers are able to reproduce the cameraman's skills with great accuracy, but we felt that on this occasion we did not want to add to the tonnage of photographic garden books dropping endlessly off the nation's presses. Photographs can brilliantly record the exact state of a garden at a given moment, and the manner in which it is planted; paintings, we feel, trade in other subtleties – such as mood, and that even less tangible experience, emotion.

For this book we have deliberately looked over our shoulders to that glorious period in Edwardian days when gardening volumes with beautiful typography and masterly bindings were further embellished by the work of such painters as Alfred Parsons (who lived and worked in Broadway) and Margaret Waterfield, a lady whose style was rapidly going out of fashion at the time of her death in the 1950s. Our written and illustrated images are personal ones; Simon has tried to avoid the expected views of the better known gardens, and I have tried to include a measure of anecdote to leaven the facts.

We have not set out to produce a guidebook to Cotswold gardens, nor is our selection meant to be by any means conclusive. When we had begun our research we became aware almost immediately that *one* book, even a very plump one, would not allow us the scope the subject demands. In the National Gardens Scheme's 'Yellow Book' there are some two hundred gardens open to the public in Gloucestershire alone – mostly in Cotswold Gloucestershire (let us ignore the name

Avon) – and then there are those numerous gardens in that part of the Cotswolds which spills into Oxfordshire.

Our final list was chosen from gardens we already knew, and from the numerous ones we visited anonymously or as invited chroniclers. Several companion volumes would be needed if we were to bring together all the gardens which deserve inclusion or, more importantly, simply appealed to us. However, our final list could, I hope, be labelled as fairly representative of the gardens in the whole region. There was only one garden where we were not made welcome, and that was because the owner wanted his beds and borders represented only through the lens of a camera.

The summer of 1990 was notable as being a particularly hot one in Britain. By July the Cotswold hills and valleys had turned beige, and in some cases trees began to defoliate long before the autumn fall. We stayed at home in Wales throughout August but returned to our list of gardens in September. No significant amount of rain had fallen during our absent month, but darker mornings with dew and mists were giving a kiss of life to parched earth, and by the time Michaelmas daisies were due many of the gardens had recovered and were able to put on a decent autumn show.

We owe a considerable debt to many people who have helped us with our tasks, and it is appropriate to thank some of them here. Others will be aware of our gratitude, not only for the time they spent shewing us their gardens (and houses), but for the remarkable hospitality offered at almost every turn. In no order of preference, we wish to thank Liz and Mark Robinson for the use of their attic bachelor quarters, ready meals, constant encouragement and kennelling arrangements; Rosemary Verey for her enthusiasm and knowledge; John and Anne Chambers and Mr Guy and the Hon. Mrs Acloque for their patience; Mary Dyer for her concern for our cuttings (and for rooting them!); the ladies at Tubby's in Nailsworth, who may never otherwise know how often their lunchtime soup kept us going; and Jim and Jean Dorrell for holding the fort in Wales during our many absences.

We saw gardens early in the morning and late in the evening; we saw them exposed to blistering sunshine and below threatening but tantalisingly dry thunder clouds. We saw ravishing gardens, mediocre gardens, even some bad gardens (by any standards). During one long summer we indulged ourselves with a rich assortment of mostly private domains, the like of which I doubt can be found anywhere else in Britain within as many square miles. Kent may have earned itself the title of being the Garden of England. The Cotswolds have *the* gardens of England.

DAVID WHEELER
May 1991

Author's Note

By taking as our title 'Over the Hills from Broadway' we are implying a certain order in which the gardens might have been seen, or a specific route meandering through the hills from the first to the last place. This was not how it happened, but for the purpose of the book we have created a running order which, roughly speaking, runs east and west from the north Cotswolds to the south.

Among the principal chapters there are four Interludes (fitting in more or less with the geographical scheme of things) bringing together images of other gardens which, because of limits of space, I have not been able to write about to the same extent. One or two smaller gardens with components which could not be ignored have also been assigned to the Interludes.

KIFTSGATE COURT

Near Chipping Campden, Gloucestershire

Depending on your approach, is it 'right' for Hidcote, or 'left' for Kiftsgate? Gardening *cognoscenti*, confronted with open gates to vastly different worlds, today turn unhesitatingly to explore the exuberant, almost riotous, 'living' garden tumbling down the escarpment towards the Vale of Evesham. The origin of one garden predates the other by only a decade and if it were not for this shared vintage and their proximity to each other, comparisons between Kiftsgate Court and Hidcote Manor would not arise. Unfruitful comparisons do occur, but the only difference which I find worth recording is that the later Kiftsgate Court garden (begun around 1920) enjoys the attentions of a young, resident descendant of its maker, while its better-known neighbour has become a museum maintained under the auspices of a corporate body. In every other respect they are incomparable.

Mr and Mrs Muir, Anne Chambers' grandparents, bought Kiftsgate Court in 1918. Belying its Georgian front, the house was built only in 1887–91. The classical façade was brought to the site from nearby Mickleton Manor by a specially-built light railway – these were pioneering days, when undaunted Victorian architects tackled projects which even with today's machinery and technology seem immensely problematical.

Heather Muir attacked these wind-blown acres with determination, working first on those parts of the garden which today incorporate the Yellow and the Rose Borders. A few years later the obligatory tennis court was added, without which it seems no country house of the 1920s and '30s could exist, and the surviving yew hedge dates from that period. Mrs Muir of course knew Lawrence Johnston across the road at Hidcote Manor, and he will doubtless have contributed some ideas to her schemes; he also painted a flower mural on an interior wall, but this now hangs in the tea-room at Hidcote. In the early 1950s the National Trust set up a local committee to oversee the management of Hidcote Manor garden, and Mrs Muir was on this committee, which worked with Graham Stuart Thomas, the Trust's garden adviser at that time.

Long before Kiftsgate Court opened to the public Graham Thomas himself wrote about the garden, in 1951, praising Mrs Muir for her 'skilled colour work'. A few years later Arthur Hellyer was trumpeting her achievements in *Amateur Gardening*, saying 'There is nothing of the wilderness here and one is immediately conscious that everything is in its place and is there for a definite purpose. That purpose is to produce a series of pictures in colour that are rich but never glaring.' When one considers most peoples' ease of mobility today, and the abundance of nurseries and garden centres, this was indeed a remarkable achievement.

Happily for Kiftsgate Diany Binny, Anne Chambers' mother, inherited from *her* mother a passion for plants and gardens as well as the house and garden itself. Here perhaps was a freer, more romantic spirit: 'How exciting to have a ruin, a grand ruin complete with Palladian portico in the middle of the garden. It would be so easy to take the roof off Kiftsgate, allowing the yellow *banksian* rose to weep over the top and perhaps meet up inside with the wisteria. No longer would one have to cut the huge-leaved *Magnolia delavayi* away from the windows, and perhaps . . . the 'Kiftsgate' rose would seize its chance to overpower all around and cover the ramparts of a Sleeping Beauty palace.'

Well, the roof stayed on, and in the garden the 'Kiftsgate' rose has reached staggering dimensions. But what is this fabled 'Kiftsgate' rose that everyone wants to have dangling merrily from their apple tree on the lawn? Present-day visitors to the garden will have noted its capabilities and not, I hope, taken away rooted cuttings and planted them to run up anything other than a robust forest tree. The plant in question, a variety of *Rosa filipes* discovered by Ernest Wilson in western China in 1908, spreads in a mound at Kiftsgate Court to some eighty by ninety feet about the base of a copper beech, and it climbs

The Temple, Kiftsgate Court

more than fifty feet into its branches – and that's *with* pruning, or, more correctly, hacking! This specimen is claimed to be the largest rose in England. Even W. J. Bean understates its possibilities in a cautionary note in his *Trees and Shrubs Hardy in the British Isles*: 'R. *filipes* . . . grows slowly at first if planted under the branches of its intended host, but gains in vigour once its stems reach the sun.'

Diany Binny has now moved to the lodge, making way for *her* daughter and family to occupy the house, but her name lives on in the garden, attached as it is to a 'half child' of the great 'Kiftsgate' rose which occurred as a seedling on 'a dirty north bank' some years ago.

Kiftsgate Court remained a private world unseen by paying visitors until 1971. Heather Muir had by then died and Diany Binny, reluctant to change things at first, gradually pulled the garden together again. She felt, as every gardener must, that changes do need to be made. And in turn Anne Chambers has had to make *her* changes as surely as *her* children will when *she* has 'gone to the lodge'.

The grass along one side of the flat entrance drive leading to the house is packed with daffodils in spring. A glimpse from the road, however, will have made visitors aware of the terrain and they will know that on their near side the land begins to fall away down the escarpment which forms the western boundary of the Cotswolds. Below them, to be explored later on foot, is the Bluebell Wood where hundreds of thousands of native bulbs completely smother the woodland floor in May.

With the garden plan in hand it is easy to find your way around Kiftsgate's tiered walkways, and the map will ensure that you leave no hidden part unexplored. Almost immediately paths open up, and with this garden's peculiar ability to absorb crowds you will find that even on the busiest afternoons you may have whole stretches of it to yourself.

I became acquainted with *Salvia candelabra* for the first time in this garden, in the Four Squares immediately in front of the classical portico. Its long bluey-mauve flowering stems riot away in high summer among groups of strong-pink 'Rita' roses. I now grow this sage in Wales, propagated from cuttings at the end of the season as I am suspicious of its ability to withstand the cold. Earlier, peonies will have played their tune in the Four Squares, and over the months to come the smart ribbed leaves of *Rodgersia pinnata* 'Superba' will have made their own special note.

The imposing walls of the house which embrace this terrace support some remarkably well-grown climbers. Delicate-looking *Rosa banksiae*, for instance, dripping with thousands of small double yellow flowers in early summer, and *Rosa chinensis* 'Mutabilis', which according to David Austin will reach eight feet, but here towers to twenty feet or more, displaying wantonly its 'pointed copper-flame buds open[ing] to single copper-yellow flowers of butterfly daintiness, soon turning to pink and finally almost crimson' (David Austin again). The *Magnolia delavayi* allowed to romp so temptingly through the windows in Diany Binny's romantic dreams covers its own part of the wall displaying 'parchment coloured, creamy-white, slightly scented flowers' in the late summer months. Mounds of choisya and *Ceanothus* 'Puget Blue' billow in warm sunshine below the sand-coloured columns rising from the balcony balustrading.

On the other side of the house the White Sunk Garden is a

The garden front, Kiftsgate Court

protected spot on a blowy day. Wise advantage is taken of its sheltered conditions and the enfolded space, complete now with octagonal raised pool, has the southern or eastern atmosphere of an enclosed courtyard. This garden no longer hosts only white flowers, although many of the plants here do produce pale blossoms which again enhance the feeling of being in a far-off place. The rare *Staphylea colchica* with long erect panicles of sweet-smelling white flowers in May is a good example of excellent plant-placing; so, too, the evergreen *Carpenteria californica* which appreciates a warm spot, as does its New Zealand companion, *Hoheria lyalii*, also with white midsummer flowers. Among the first to show their heads in this area, before Easter usually, are the double forms of *Sanguinaria canadensis* whose name refers to their beet-fleshed roots, not their chalky white flowers. Trilliums and little erythroniums (dog's-tooth violets) belong to the same season.

Heather Muir also has a rose named for her. Again it is a chance seedling found here and recognised as a worthwhile hybrid – of *R. sericea*, this time. It has numerous, pure white single flowers, and grows to twelve feet or so without any staking or support.

In the summer there is a noticeable increase in colour in this small garden; another herbaceous plant carries a reference to blood in its name, *Potentilla astrosanguinea*, and alstroemerias make a cloud of coral-pink blossom under the rose 'Pax', appropriately named to mark the end of the First World War and, coincidentally of course, the year when the Muirs arrived at Kiftsgate Court.

One of the most striking features in this garden, and one of the very few formal elements, is the long pair of hedges of two-tone 'Rosa Mundi', sport of *Rosa gallica officinalis*, seen first through an archway cut in a wall of copper beech. Their striped petals of dark and paler pink are dramatic in themselves, and here at Kiftsgate some of the bushes are reverting to single-colour plants whose occasional dark heads punctuate the two rows with a greater intensity of colour. The rose hedges are pruned to stay roughly knee-high. They have a grass path between them leading to a new piece of sculpture by Simon Verity framed in an unusual arc of clipped whitebeam, *Sorbus aria* 'Lutescens', whose unfolding new white leaves can be easily mistaken at a distance for magnolia flower buds. A short time ago when I wanted to plant for myself a formal hedge of clipped whitebeams, I was advised by an expert that this tree would not take fondly to the required severe pruning; Anne Chambers tells me this arch is six or seven years old now, and the plants appear healthy enough. Perhaps sorrow is being stored up; I hope not, for this is a stroke of genius, the planting emphasised further by a backdrop of tall dark yew hedging.

The long flower borders all appear to perch on the north and north-west edge of the garden with glimpses through them to the Vale beyond. Each is thickly planted, and where there are shrubs too these seem to blend in with the lower limbs of mature trees creating thickets of flowery spikes and branches. The Wide Border presents itself in shades of mauve and purple, crimson and pink, leavened with bountiful heaps of grey foliage. Several species and hybrid lilies thrust through mats of campanulas and herbaceous geraniums hooking themselves onto rose thorns, conjuring the sort of sensual

Whitebeam arch, Kiftsgate Court

midsummer images that would have inspired many of the artists living around Broadway and Chipping Campden at the turn of the century.

The Yellow Border relies as much on 'golden' foliage as on yellow flowers. Pure blue delphiniums, randomly strewn, pull the range of hues together, unifying just one rib of the spectrum, while closer analysis reveals tones from the palest lemon to bright orange. It is fitting that David Austin's 'Graham Thomas', a yellow-flowered Modern Shrub rose raised in 1983, finds a place here.

From the North Border, under tall Scotch pines which have witnessed a century of spiteful gales, steps begin to lead through a series of zig-zag paths to the Lower Garden. On emerging as from a dark tunnel, visitors find themselves in a new world of ordered chaos sweeping round the great curve of a semi-circular lawn held briefly by a ha-ha before the landscape falls again down the slopes to the vast plain, with distant views of the whaleback Malvern Hills.

The family swimming pool is situated in the lower area, and the poolhouse used for changing has been built to mimic a small Grecian temple, half hidden in early summer in a grove of self-seeded blue and white abutilons. On the right day, not too hot, with sluggish clouds letting through enough sunshine to illuminate the abstract pattern of yellow rape-filled fields disappearing westwards halfway to Wales, there can be no better place to sit and to reflect, perhaps, on how this bewitching scene came to be assembled. The luxuriant but casual planting surely caused frequent aching backs, broken finger nails, and sleepless nights wondering how many young shoots were being devoured by pesky rabbits. When people say that a garden is as much for sitting in as toiling over, this is what they have in mind – tranquillity, fragrance, rampant but subdued colour within sight of well-cared-for rolling farmland. This is not unique to the Cotswolds, but it becomes an increasingly endangered scene in a modern world.

Among the abutilons, bamboos and grasses, lilies and ribbons of alchemilla, can be found another carpenteria, tree peonies and *Magnolia hypoleuca*, handsome in both flower and fruit. At the feet of the slope are tender *Geranium maderense* with huge bright-pink flower heads, and tufts of shoulder-high euphorbias whose acid-green bracts are spiked here and there with tall, cobalt-blue irises.

Climbing back to the top garden by a different path you will pass a small pool where variegated flag irises shine out in the shade of overhanging pines. The woodland path is littered with fuchsias and jewel-like yellow and orange Welsh poppies (*Meconopsis cambrica*), as bright as broken pieces of coloured cathedral glass.

Anne and John Chambers have undertaken considerable new plantings throughout the steep banks. The soil is poor but this seems not to have handicapped them, and the resulting mass of plants will help to stabilise the slopes and prevent erosion and possible land-slides.

Thankfully the Chamberses propagate many of their plants, and very often there is a good selection to choose from by the front door. Anne puts up a board displaying coloured photographs of most of her plants so that customers can recall what they have seen in the garden,

Mask, at the pool-side, Kiftsgate Court

or perhaps be tempted to try a plant which was 'out of season' at the time of their visit.

From Muir to Binny to Chambers, this garden has descended down the green-fingered distaff side of a decidedly horticultural family. Anne and John have at present two sons and one daughter; which of these, one wonders, will be the distinguished, fourth-generation Kiftsgate gardener?

HIDCOTE MANOR

Near Chipping Campden, Gloucestershire

The two most potent words in English gardening language are Sissinghurst and Hidcote. Vita Sackville-West with her husband Harold Nicolson (the latter not always credited for his masterly design), joint creators of the garden at Sissinghurst Castle, and Lawrence Johnston, a shy American bachelor who made the garden at Hidcote Manor, would appear at first glance to have had little in common. Yet, in almost successive decades and two hundred miles apart, they built two gardens that have established themselves firmly near the top of the garden-visiting charts, with reputations stretching around the world.

The history of each garden is amply documented, but it is worth recalling here the ghost of Major Johnston, whose influence on garden design over almost a century is far greater than he could have ever hoped, imagined or, possibly, wanted.

He was born in Paris in 1871. His mother, Gertrude Waterbury, from one of America's top 'Four Hundred' families, was brought up on the fashionable side of New York City. She married Elliot Johnston, a Maryland banker's son, the year before Lawrence's birth. Mrs Johnston was soon bereaved of a second son, a baby daughter and then her husband. But in 1887 she married again and became the wife of Charles Winthrop, a wealthy East Coast barrister who had taken to living away from his native land. The marriage ended in 1898 with Mr Winthrop's death, the year after Lawrence came down from Trinity College, Cambridge with a degree in history.

After Lawrence Johnston took British citizenship (in order to fight in the Boer War) Mrs Winthrop bought for her son a farm in

Northumberland so that he could be near an army colleague with whom he had made a special friendship. But the cold hills of northern England, apparently devoid of the society for which Mrs Winthrop seems to have been bred, were unable to hold her. Further south, in the Cotswolds, around Broadway in particular, Mrs Winthrop's antennae detected a thriving community of artists and socialites which included fellow Americans. She learnt of an estate for sale of 300 acres including farmhouse and hamlet, and successfully bid for it at auction in July 1907. Hidcote Bartrim, five miles from Broadway, was set for transformation and fame.

Their 'neighbours' were the painter Alfred Parsons and the architect Charles Bateman. There was Mary Anderson de Navarro at Court Farm, Captain Simpson Hayward (founder of the Alpine Garden Society) at Icomb, Rose Berkeley (sister of ill-fated Ellen Willmott who bankrupted herself in the name of horticulture) at Spetchley Park near Worcester, and George Lees-Milne whose topiary garden was at nearby Wickhamford. Sargent, Elgar and Burne-Jones drifted through the charmed circle.

William Morris's Society for the Protection of Ancient Buildings, and the Arts and Crafts revival, were firmly established. Hidcote Bartrim's farmhouse was restored and renamed Hidcote Manor and Lawrence Johnston, then in his mid-thirties, threw all his energies into horticulture.

The garden at Hidcote Manor consists of many compartments or 'garden rooms', enclosed mainly by tall yew hedges. It is perched on the Cotswold escarpment, overlooking the Vale of Evesham, where without its screens and hedges it would be blasted by every mischievous storm.

My first visit was in 1986 when I was invited to lunch by an American gentleman and his wife who had been enjoying a series of short midsummer vacations at the Manor during Sir Gawain and Lady Bell's regular spells of absence. It was a warm day, firmly fixed in my mind (or, rather, nostrils) by that year's first bout of hayfever, but I sneezed my way through the garden pushing my nose into every rose and lily I encountered. I was able to enjoy the garden and discover its many unexpected turns and fancies without tripping over or bumping into countless visitors with their cameras at the ready, waiting for that precious moment when the sun emerges from behind a wayward cloud, or that even rarer instance when a particularly pleasing frame is not masked by two plumply-filled white cardigans.

I was of course aware of the criticisms which this garden has attracted, namely its state of over-tidiness and a curious lack of soul, but on this glorious first occasion I felt I recognised some of the heart and spirit which have caused writers, even during the garden's infancy, to reach eagerly for their inkwells. It was a great privilege to wander those paths without disruption, and it was good of the National Trust to allow Simon Dorrell and me to have the place to ourselves again for an afternoon in March last year.

Lawrence Johnston began on raw farming land; there was no garden for him to respond to – he was able to start absolutely from scratch, without any regard for an existing plan or other men's ideas.

Here is grand formality reduced to what is essentially an English cottage garden or series of cottage gardens, albeit on a scale that most cottagers would fight shy of. The 'rooms' of box and yew nearest the house have themes of their own, and although this is not the place to describe them in guidebook manner, it is appropriate to give some indication of the many styles which, with outrageous success, the Major attempted.

Vita Sackville-West must not be remembered as the inventor of the so-called 'white garden, even though her example at Sissinghurst Castle is perhaps the most satisfying and beautiful of all 'single-colour' gardens: here at Hidcote Manor Lawrence Johnston made a White Garden years before the Nicolsons acquired their legendary domain. It is situated under a cedar of Lebanon whose huge branches form a majestic canopy.

The Fuchsia Garden, with low 'walls' of clipped box, is planted in the spring with light blue scillas packed into its eight beds next to the Pool Garden, where a raised disc of water leaves only just enough room to walk between its low ivy-clad rim and the great encircling hedge of clipped yew. Two brick-built gazebos at the end of the Red Borders mark a change in level where steps lead up to the Stilt Garden, a *palissade à l'italienne* whose pleached hornbeams create an elegant structure of green architecture through which can be glimpsed a magnificent pair of ornamental iron gates calling you to come and admire the timeless views across the Vale.

The Fuchsia Garden in April, Hidcote Manor

If, like me, you can enjoy exploring a garden without a map (although it is essential with a garden like this to see it again with the benefit of a plan), there are many surprises in store at Hidcote Manor. The Long Walk, so delightfully seen first through the open doors of the gazebo, made me want to walk to its far end and return the same way. But what happened? I crossed a low grassed bridge, saw a previously-unsighted stream running at right angles to and *below* the Walk, and found myself strolling in an entirely new direction to discover the woodland harmony which flows from this part of the garden out into open countryside. This was the pleasure of a non-intellectual approach to the garden, and one that I feel could be repeated on subsequent visits.

The planting at Hidcote Manor is excellent. There are in almost every case the best forms of any species or cultivar. There is part of the National Collection of peonies (species and primary hybrids) in the

The Stilt Garden, Spring, Hidcote Manor

Pillar Garden (the pillars being formed of yew on square yew bases); long herbaceous borders in the Kitchen Garden filled to bursting in summer but a treat earlier in the year too, and the Old Garden where plants with soft colours in shades of pink and mauve and pale yellows and blues are grown.

Despite his adopted 'Englishness' and his beautifully crafted garden, Lawrence Johnston never shunned the outside world. He went on two important plant-collecting expeditions: the first, in 1927, to South Africa from Cape Town to the Victoria Falls with Captain Collingwood ('Cherry') Ingram and George (later Sir George) Taylor with whom he climbed into the Drakensburg Mountains, resulted in a collection of plants being sent to the Edinburgh Botanic Garden.

On a second more gruelling trip in 1931, then aged sixty, he accompanied the Scotsman George Forrest on what was to be his (Forrest's) last journey. On this occasion Major Johnston fell ill and returned early.

Lawrence Johnston also loved the France of his birth. In the early 1920s he travelled south with his mother and rented a villa near the sanatorium where, suffering senile dementia, Mrs Winthrop later became a patient. In 1924 he bought Serre de la Madonne, a villa on the Riviera at Menton near the Italian border, and over a few years increased its acreage by buying up land from his neighbours. Mrs Winthrop died there in 1926. Eventually Lawrence forsook the north Cotswolds, settling on the Mediterranean where he was able to grow many plants that had refused to oblige him in Gloucestershire. In 1948 he made arrangements for Hidcote Manor to be passed to the National Trust, who had agreed to accept it under its new Gardens Scheme. He died in 1958, aged 87. His body was brought back to England and buried next to his mother's in Mickleton churchyard, just a few miles from the famous garden he created out of windswept Cotswold upland.

Hidcote Manor survives to this day, polished and tidged to within an inch of its life and a 'victim' now of around 100,000 visitors a year. American Indians once believed that when an image of them was taken by a camera, part of their soul was taken as well. If the Major's masterpiece seems these days to be lacking *its* soul, then perhaps we should consider what has been removed from this garden by too many pairs of feet, too many rolls of film and, oh dear, too many pages of print.

SNOWSHILL MANOR

Snowshill, Gloucestershire

For me, Snowshill Manor could be the perfect home. It consists of a warm-coloured stone house and ancient outbuildings, comfortable-looking and manageable in every way, set in a quiet, almost remote, north Cotswold village and protected from outside prying eyes by sturdy walls of sensitive proportions.

In 1919 the architect Charles Paget Wade (1883–1956) must have thought much the same. Having seen an advertisement for the dilapidated fifteenth-century house he secured a freehold, and in a remarkably short time had divided up the grounds with low walls of the same local stone to create a superbly structured garden with quirky angles, on several levels. He was led by friend and fellow-architect Hugh Baillie Scott (1865–1945), a man whose principles insisted upon an inseparable relationship between house and garden. Scott had worked independently on London's Hampstead Garden Suburb, while Wade was a member of Raymond Unwin's architectural team engaged on the same project.

At Snowshill Manor they constructed staged but unexpected glimpses of village houses and church to be seen through gates or over walls, and they created simple 'story-book' views of the ravishing countryside framed by grand gate-piers topped with stately stone balls.

Much of the unity of the place comes from the use of a particular shade of blue paint applied to gates, wooden planting tubs, seats, and general trim. It is an almost daring use of colour, but a shade wholly complementary to the stone and to the many hues of foliage-greens and a spectrum of flower colours to sate the most demanding of horticultural connoisseurs.

The entrance to the house, with plain rectangles of flat lawn each side of a gravel path, opens up beyond a woodland approach of the severest contrast. From a dark, mysterious glade you walk, not drive, into a sunny courtyard that does nothing to distract from the elegant south façade of the house, which somehow contrives a homely feeling despite its strict lines of 'classical' symmetry. The high wall separating the property from the street is dressed with roses, ceanothus and clematis with lavender at their feet.

The garden levels drop by slopes and terraces from the west side of the house. Below a wall festooned with pink valerian lies the Armillary Court, so named for its centrally-placed stone column bearing an armillary sphere consisting of bands of gilded metal. Tall cones of Irish yew, and their dramatic shadows on sunny days, flank the eastern wall.

Another courtyard, the Well Court, is paved in the softest-coloured stone around the sunken pool containing a few water-lilies. Square blue-painted tubs each holding a fastigiate juniper stand at the four corners. This courtyard is enclosed on two sides by single-storey buildings whose roofs are clad in the graded stone tiles (the deepest at the eaves, the narrowest at the ridge) which can be seen throughout the Cotswolds. A carved figure of the Virgin Mary, set into a dormer on the Garden House roof, suggests a monastic mood of stillness and peace.

Stone has a responsible and varied function in this garden: random pieces in walls are often smothered with aubrietia as well as outcrops of valerian and other plants that enjoy a dry root run. Where dressed, the same stone embellishes the house, the outbuildings and numerous incidental details.

But there are plenty of flowers, too, in borders and in grass. Spring bulbs are well distributed in the turf, bringing the garden into bloom with bright yellow daffodils long before leaves emerge on the overhead trees. Blue scillas and celandines carpet the grass in the Guelder Rose Grove during the early months, while autumn brings hardy cyclamen springing from corms now grown to the size of tea-plates.

The main flower border is unusually placed and it could be assumed to lie outside the garden's bounds: south facing, it runs in two very long narrow beds between the high wall on one side of the Armillary

Irises, Snowshill Manor

Court and the apple orchard, which in itself seems just to run away and become lost in the open wold. The National Trust describes the planting in these borders as 'deliberately unsophisticated'. These words hardly do justice to the glorious profusion of flowers falling over themselves and interweaving among the lower stems of rampant wall shrubs and climbers, including espaliered fruit trees, figs, clematis and roses. It is interesting to note that this wall is made, or rather faced, with brick, the other side being stone – a common feature in old kitchen gardens, where walls were required to warm up early in the day, soak up as much of the sun's heat as possible, and give it back at night to ward off slight frosts early in the season and advance the ripening process later. Both Kiftsgate Court and Stowell Park have brick-lined kitchen garden walls to provide the home-grown apricots and figs once required to enhance the dining-room table.

'Snozzle', as it is affectionately known, is full of harmonious elements: its peaceful setting, its strong but never fussy design, its planting, crisp and pure in some places, riotous and romantic in others, all add up to an achievement both grand and relaxed, inspired *and* inspiring.

As long ago as 1520 George Cavendish, a gentleman of Thomas Wolsey's household and the author of a remarkable biography of the cardinal, wrote some verses describing Hampton Court gardens. The twentieth-century maker of Snowshill's garden borrowed two (non-consecutive) lines from this work and painted them on a 'Wade-blue' board between two gate piers:

> My garden sweet enclosed with walls strong
> The arbours and allees so pleasant and so dulce

They speak well of Mr Wade's ambitions and his achievements. He must have been very happy here.

MR AND MRS IAN BOND

UPTON WOLD

Near Moreton-in-Marsh, Gloucestershire

This most beautiful of houses, built in the early 1600s, seems untouched by time. We all know, though, or can imagine, what four hundred years of weather can do to a building, and what we see at Upton Wold today is a masterpiece of restoration by its present owners. In a decade and a half they have also laid out around the house a large garden of botanical and horticultural delight. The hilly character of the north Cotswold countryside rolls up to the walls of the house, and I would suggest that eschewing any attempt to level it all out has been one of the master-strokes of this garden's creation.

This is the high Cotswolds, cold and exposed, but the house sits cleverly in a hollow, its roof and chimneys away from the world's attention.

When Ian and Caroline Bond came here the house was surrounded by their predecessor's messy cabbage plots, without a hint of any ornamental garden. They have performed what amounts almost to a miracle. In the formal forecourt they have made the simplest of welcoming entrances by screening from sight all views of the remarkable garden, and contenting themselves with well-kept lawns each side of a gravel path, a row of clipped box shapes gently enlivening the walls of the building which forms a right angle to the spectacular façade of the house. In sharp contrast, on the bank opposite there is a grove of walnut trees with generous scatterings of daffodils and wild flowers through which paths are cut leading to a Pond Garden quite hidden from anyone's eyes. Only farmland lies beyond.

As I am always curious to learn how people approach what appear to be unsurmountable problems, I was surprised by Caroline Bond's

The house, Upton Wold

remark that her first move was to erect a Cambridge greenhouse large enough to provide a year-round supply of flowers for the house. To this day she grows orchids, cyclamen, azaleas, scented rhododendrons and pots of bulbs, as well as flowers for cutting.

The attack on the garden was, however, almost simultaneous. In the mid-1970s Mr and Mrs Bond invited the then 78-year-old Brenda Colvin, CBE (1897–1981) to come and advise on the part of the garden known today as the East Terrace Borders. Her immediate and striking insistence was that the magnificent view *must* be preserved, and that any landscaping *must* respect this view for all time. Her words were heeded, and with high yew hedges now framing that particular aspect I can only assume that if Miss Colvin could revisit Upton Wold today, she would walk happily along its grass paths and admire the influence that Hal Moggridge, her last professional partner, has continued to effect.

Miss Colvin's plans for the East Terrace Borders survive, and most of the original planting is extant. White-flowering exochordas proved unsatisfactory and have been removed, but the overall picture still largely represents her specification. She defined the area with hedges and suggested small groups of roses ('Constance Spry', 'Blanc Double de Coubert', *R. rubrifolia*, 'Cardinal de Richelieu') interspersed with viburnums, *Fatsia japonica*, *Magnolia kobus* at one end, all underplanted with the likes of *Lilium regale*, white japanese anemones, hellebores, fritillaries, crocuses, sedums, *Anemone blanda*, foxgloves (*Digitalis ambigua*), pinks, geraniums and lavender. This wide-ranging list demonstrates perfectly the scope of the planting which, with *Mahonia japonica* and *Viburnum* × *bodnantense* 'Dawn' for midwinter colour, provides flowers virtually throughout the year. To Brenda Colvin's original plants Mrs Bond has added her own subtle touches here and there by introducing a calycanthus, wintersweet, some tree peonies (including 'King of White Lion' among others she imported from Japan, and 'Mrs William Kelway'). The two borders run left from the terrace and curve slightly, imposing a sense of mystery, and at the same time make an unsuspected path to a point revealing a dramatic view of a very long, tapering border which, like a streak, runs down a gentle slope between a stone wall and a high yew hedge.

At the corner where Miss Colvin's borders and the Herbaceous Walk meet there is a stone seat in its own box bay, with the sound of spring water gurgling behind its left shoulder. Ian Bond relishes the sound of water in the garden, and the splashes from this spout not only add a musical note but help keep a group of primulas and hostas properly damp. This long border, about twelve feet wide at the top, is in three distinct sections with strong colours at the near end fading through the spectrum to white some one hundred yards away; not a single blade of grass could penetrate the thick tapestry in high summer. For height there are delphiniums, Michaelmas daisies, rudbeckias, golden rods and crambe. Less high are campanulas, eryngiums, a selection of different comfreys, herbaceous peonies, and poppies. Weaving around their feet are hardy geraniums, cornflowers, alchemilla, penstemons and catmint. Stepping stones run along the back of the border to allow the gardener access for pruning and tidying the climbers which deck the wall. The border is so well planted that the grading of herbaceous flowers rises into the wall climbers; these include the roses 'Paul's Lemon Pillar' and 'Albertine', *Clematis*

The Herbaceous Walk, Upton Wold

tibetana, C. × *jouiniana, C. cirrhosa* var. *balearica,* and the dark cultivar 'Niobe'. There are honeysuckles, too, and ceanothus, and the curious South American *Araujia sericofera* or Cruel Plant, so named for the way its strongly-scented flowers attract then trap night-flying insects by the tongue. Although each of the three sections of this border enjoys its own range of graded colours, the unifying effect of a low edging of dark 'Hidcote' lavender runs for the entire length. The border comes to a definite stop with a cloud of white *Romneya coulteri* and white rosebay willow-herb (*Epilobium angustifolium* 'Album') under *Malus toringoides*. If your attention wanders slightly as you make your progression down this border, you may catch a glimpse of another part of the garden through 'windows', devised by Mr Moggridge, cut in the right-hand yew hedge.

The view through the 'windows' is of one of the very few level parts of the garden which, in two lawned tiers seen from the Terrace, lets the eye race out of the garden to revel in the perspective of that folding countryside which Brenda Colvin was so anxious to preserve.

In a small arbour composed of an existing retaining buttress for a wall and a block of yew are the scented, double-flowered 'Duchess of Edinburgh' clematis and 'Paul's Himalayan Musk' rose. This is the only flowery embellishment to the lawn, its understatement making a powerful contribution. Behind and on a higher level is a 'secret' yew walk or tunnel, terminated by a classical figure on a plinth – another example of the way surprises have been tucked into the design of this garden.

From a small opening off the lawn you can enter the Hidden Garden, a mass of shrubby plants surrounding a tilting disc of grass with a centrally-placed statue of Mercury. An almost solid wall of glossy-leaved, evergreen *Phillyrea angustifolia* marks the entrance point, and on the left under a spreading old apple tree (with the white, tea-scented rose 'Mrs Herbert Stevens' climbing through its branches) is a swarming patch of snowdrops and lily-of-the-valley to sweeten the springtime air. A stone seat, thoughtfully placed for a summer visitor's momentary relaxation, lies against the wall. There are some excellent shrubs and small trees in the Hidden Garden: a still-young but tall paulownia, a weeping caragana with pea-like flowers, several magnolias including *M. highdownensis* – grown originally from seedlings raised by the late Sir Frederick Stern in his Sussex garden, from a batch received in the late 1920s from Caerhays Castle in Cornwall; and *M. sinensis*, a tough Chinese species with white, lemon-scented, downward-facing flowers. The underplanting comprises low hebes, shrubby honeysuckles, Himalayan blue poppies (meconopsis) and *Digitalis* × *mertonensis*, a foxglove whose flowers Graham Stuart Thomas describes beautifully as having 'a strange tint of rosy mauve, shot with coppery-buff'.

By a screen of bamboo, *Arundinaria japonica*, you begin to climb into the old orchard whose remaining elderly denizens now find themselves invaded by glorious, exotic trees from far corners of the world. The prize among them is the yellow-flowered magnolia from the eastern United States, *M. acuminata*, with young fruit clusters which have given it the common name of Cucumber Tree. Also in the orchard now are *Davidia involucrata*, *Parrotia persica*, and a wing-nut, *Pterocarya fraxinifolia*, a member of the walnut family which puts on very speedy growth to become a mature-looking tree within two decades. A row of young amelanchiers, underplanted with bluebells, runs up one side of the orchard to an old 'Chanticleer' pear, and among the full-summer, leafy boughs of the older trees Ian Bond has cut a *claire-voie* to frame another ravishing glimpse of the land beyond. Among the orchard grass are very old clumps of daffodils which a village woman, now ninety, can remember seeing in profusion as a young girl.

The route we have taken brings us now to a high, fairly flat level where large fruit cages protect rows of strawberries and raspberries. Box hedges and espaliered apples edge the soft fruit, and a narrow border runs beside an old Cotswold-stone stock barrier where flowers – peonies, foxgloves, irises, blue and white agapanthus, Canterbury bells and cowslips – are grown for cutting. Because of the exposed position in this part of the garden, the Bonds have broken into an adjoining field to plant a shelter belt whose more common components are larch and beech. But with an eye to always making every part of the garden look as good as it can, this screen of useful trees has been interplanted with white-flowering cherries and silvery-leaved whitebeams.

The approach to this top level can also be made through an imposing pair of gate-piers set at the head of a broad grass ride rising from the tiered lawn and carrying on out through the shelter belt to the open fields. Another low Cotswold-stone wall, to the right of the piers, is ribboned with a border of tightly-packed blue, rhizomatous irises which last year yielded over three hundred and fifty blooms. Opposite this long border is a vegetable-growing area, finished at one end with a low hedge of white lavender, roses for cutting, and standard-grown honeysuckles with an embellishment of variegated hollies, every ten feet or so, being trained into spheres on bare stems. This part of the garden is coming together very decoratively, and is distinct in every way from the kind of formal *potager* to be seen at Barnsley House. The scale here is different, it is less intensively cultivated, and there is a freedom of planting which leaves great scope for further ideas to be incorporated.

Descending again into the garden which seems to enfold the house on all sides, there is the original Kitchen Garden where, even in winter, there are pleasing rows of grey artichokes to admire. The Herb Garden, within the Kitchen Garden, has zig-zag partitions of box hedging which create an attractive formal pattern and also help to segregate some of the more wayward herbs, and prevent others from falling into each other. Three short, narrow borders lead off from the main path of the Kitchen Garden to a range of former cattle sheds which have been transformed to rooms where parties and shooting lunches can be held. These borders have low-growing, mainly blue and white flowers like aquilegias, forget-me-nots and the smaller kinds of spring bulbs, to cover the ground beneath apple trees trained into screens dividing the paths. More apples, the crab 'John Downie', form a long tunnel out of the Kitchen Garden and are underplanted with 'Cream Beauty' crocuses to be followed almost immediately by blue *Scilla siberica* in the early months.

Here again we turn, into another large area which abuts the orchard. By the four-square, listed dovecot we enter a sloping site with large beds planted mainly with shrubs to give a semi-wild, bosky effect. *Cotoneaster franchetii*, *Prunus spinosa* 'Purpurea' (a blackthorn, or sloe, cultivar), *Salix hookeriana* and *Cornus alba* 'Elegantissima' are among the shrubs whose general range of colours is pink and grey. The Peony Border runs along the wall, contained by a serpentine box hedge. The mostly pink and white, some double, peonies are mixed in with hellebores, and aquilegias in shades of blue and white. Another of the large island beds on the slope has a white theme, the shrubs underplanted with more hellebores and small-leaved white lamiums. An unusual shrub here is *Deutzia setchuenensis corymbiflora*, whose long-lasting flowers appear in early July and continue well into September.

Two beds of hazels, with their catkins showing at the same time as

The Kitchen Garden, Upton Wold

the flowers of the polyanthus and narcissi below them, are given a certain touch of refinement by the addition of clipped box balls around the edges. It is little gestures like these which give so much extra pleasure to what might otherwise appear as quite ordinary pieces of woodland planting. Everywhere in this garden you are aware of human hands having worked – sometimes discreetly – to improve upon the condition in which many other gardeners would have been happy to let things rest. Such extra 'push' is among the many practices which lift this garden into a very special class.

A particularly steep slope forms the approach to the west side of the house, and here Caroline Bond wanted to avoid terracing which she feels would not have been sympathetic to the house, or appropriate to the style of landscaping which might have been carried out when the house was built. Her solution was to devise a series of beds, designed by Hal Moggridge, which give the appearance of massed roses having been 'flung across the bank'. Four large beds, each different but of precisely the right shape and scale, now occupy this slope. The beds are so well wedded to their site that a returning stroll to the house seems a mere gradual descent. In most cases the beds are planted quite closely with six or nine roses of the same variety, tied to wire hoops to prevent them growing too high and becoming untidy, and spoiling the low, mounded effect. For the period in the year before leaves appear on the roses there is a carefully-considered scheme of plants to bring early colour. Snowdrops, winter aconites, crocuses and hellebores do the work simply and imaginatively. The roses, in their bold groups, include 'Fritz Nobis', 'Petite de Hollande', 'Madame Pierre Oger', 'Queen of Denmark', 'Maiden's Blush', 'Fru Dagmar Hastrup', *R. moyesii* 'Geranium' (with conspicuous heps), *R. macrantha*, 'Sissinghurst Castle', 'Cécile Brunner', 'Félicité Parmentier', *R.* 'Paulii', 'Tuscany Superb', 'Madame Hardy', 'Fantin Latour' and at least a dozen others. The midsummer appearance, and fragrance, can be easily imagined. At the top of the rose bank there are white lilacs and *Philadelphus* 'Belle Etoile' contrasting with a dark green, wavy-topped hedge of *Lonicera nitida*.

Hal Moggridge has also made a warm, raised bed near the Billiard Room door, above a small courtyard where the family can eat and entertain during good weather. Cistuses and *Ceanothus repens* enjoy the well-drained soil, and a nicely-placed rosemary bush has to be brushed against when one ascends the steps – thereby releasing its distinctive aromatic fragrance.

Around the warm walls of this west side of the house are beds with named varieties of alstroemerias, a yellow banksian rose, actinidia, choisya, piptanthus, *Carpenteria californica*, jasmine and phlomis. In summer there are pots of oleanders (overwintered in the greenhouse) and tubs of blue felicias, glaucous, cut-leaved melianthus and white daisy-like argyranthemums.

The greenhouse, heated in winter, contains the sort of collection of unusual plants that any private and some botanical gardens might envy. Scented gladiolus with long, grass-like leaves from South Africa and a collection of nerines add extra interest to the ranks of pelargoniums, irises, and many more exotics. On a January visit I noticed in the house a vase full of white buddleia whose slender white racemes were slightly scented. In the heated greenhouse I saw the plant from which they had come; it is *Buddleia fallowiana*, cut back severely after April to encourage flowers at the turn of the year.

Ian and Caroline Bond, with their two gardeners, Theresa Jones and Ron Lloyd, have made one of the great Cotswold gardens – in a very short time. They have many plans for the future, and I have no doubt that in another fifteen years the description of the parts I have given here will form just a small proportion of a much larger garden. At present it is one of the Cotswolds' best-kept secrets.

BOURTON HOUSE

Bourton-on-the-Hill, Gloucestershire

G ardening is thoroughly *enjoyed* at Bourton House. One might say that it is pursued in an almost larky fashion, totally at odds with how one might suppose the occupants of such a gracious Queen Anne mansion to carry on. But then, this garden is full of surprises, too. Stuffiness is non-existent and the absence of a faultless flow of Latin names pouring from the owners' mouths is as refreshing (and welcome) as a cup of Earl Grey tea on a hot afternoon in a still hammock.

Canadian-born Monique Paice is young and enthusiastic, learning about plants and horticulture as she works alongside her gardeners, Paul Williams and Heather Price, who have been with the Paices at Bourton House since 1984. These two people are essential to the garden: together they form a perfect team, of inspired plantsman and indefatigable Trojan. They are adding to an established garden while preserving the very best of what was there.

The spectacularly good-looking stone-built house (described by Nicholas Kingsley as an 'unusual plan of a rectangle with four projecting corner towers') sits on the vaulted remains of a Jacobean, or earlier, dwelling, and it is possible that parts of the garden's layout may date from the late sixteenth or early seventeenth century. Perhaps the large flat lawn at the back (south side) of the house, sloping up at the far end to a wide walking-terrace many yards long, is a remnant from centuries past. Its low wall brings the garden to an abrupt stop overlooking a considerable drop, serving an identical function to the balustrading in some Italian villa gardens, where this device prevents careless strollers tumbling into the village below. The five huge, evenly-spaced terracotta pots on the terrace, spilling their bountiful nasturtiums under last year's clear summer skies, added more than a touch of southern-European atmosphere but the landscape beyond, as traditionally English as it is possible to be, lacked the silvery gleam of olive trees to complete the Italian illusion.

In every other respect, however, this is an English garden with its own pedigree: a previous owner, Colonel Head, brought in Lanning Roper in the early 1960s, and subsequent owners have gardened here with distinction.

But Richard and Monique Paice, relying heavily on Paul and Heather, have not been afraid to make changes – no new owners should be. A garden is a living thing incapable of surviving in a static state. Arguments about this have gone on for ages and everyone can nominate their own example of an otherwise beautiful garden suffocated by the great strides (or bank balances) made (or spent) in the name of preservation.

There are three acres presently gardened here, some laid to orchard. Within the garden walls, so to speak, there are herbaceous borders, shaded courtyards, an elegant new parterre, and little incidents which make you wonder if you have strayed into a meadow. On the west side of the house there is a courtyard with a small formal box-edged garden surrounding a double-basin fountain overlooked by a very tall arched window containing forty-eight panes of glass. On the walls of the house and two of its 'wings' *Pyracantha* 'Mojave', planted only four years ago, has climbed in tiers to twelve feet or so. The pleached branches follow the horizontal mortar courses with precision, and in a few years all the 'arms' will join up to create a striking embellishment.

A much larger parterre is under construction on a slightly higher piece of ground close by. Hundreds of six-inch box plants have been set in an intricate pattern to surround a large oval basin made of reconstituted stone in the shape of a shallow woven basket. Nearby there is a corner seemingly ignored except by the man with his mowing machine. An arc of cut turf lies beside a patch of unmown grass full of knee-high marguerite daisies. Eight staddle stones pull your eye round the arc to leave you gazing out over fields and trees. It is a daring trick to perform so close to the new grid of formality, but all the better for it.

Staddle stones, Bourton House

This formal area is shielded from the rest of the garden by a mixed border of predominantly grey and pink shrubs and herbaceous perennials. Opposite, on the far side of the lawn, a west-facing border is crammed with plants whose colours occupy the yellow and orange slice of the spectrum; all very refined, and just as the house deserves. However, I detected a freer and more ambitious style of planting in the short pair of borders leading out from the lawn, and there has been a great deal of activity going on as part of the old walled Kitchen Garden's transformation to an enclosed space full of colours and scents.

Monique Paice has wonderfully frank opinions of certain plants: she tolerates crambe for its marvellous foliage and white froth of flowers in midsummer despite its 'farm-yard fragrance' and inelegant manner of dying. *Crambe cordifolia* works well in the borders, filling them out to a welcome plumpness after earlier flowers have gone on their way. Associated with tall cardoons and white *Lilium candidum*, acanthus, creamy-yellow *Anthemis tinctoria* 'Wargrave Variety' and curry plants, with intensely-blue spikes of tall salvias and a few sharp-coloured penstemons, these borders are able to maintain interest over a long summer period.

The old Kitchen Garden is now bisected by a wide gravel path whose edges are invaded by the thickly-planted borders running either side. In the middle, a low-edged rectangular pool reflects the gate piers and their new black iron gates beyond which, without further interruption, the Gloucestershire countryside rolls away to distant woods. The sprawling rose 'Max Graf' inhabits the corners of the beds where they break for the pool, and rising out of these are four standard-trained 'Madame Lemoine' lilacs whose top-of-the-milk coloured flowerheads dispense a strong perfume in early summer. At right angles to the pool another path leads behind a hornbeam screen to a hot border against one of the old walls. More use of gravel intensifies the 'southern' mood which this diversely-planted border generates. Stems of *Rosa glauca* (syn. *Rosa rubrifolia*) work their way through purple-leaved sedums, and hefty clumps of *Phormium cookianum* 'Tricolor' with striped, strap-like leaves provide an extravagant contrast to the grey softness of the phlomis leaves. This is *Phlomis cashmeriana* with whorls of pale lavender flowers, not the Jerusalem sage with mustardy-yellow ones. At the far (south) end of this strip, against a high shade-giving wall, is a collection of ivies fumbling their way through and over a pile of boulders.

Table produce has not been ousted simply because the old Kitchen Garden has been given new blood. In a small formal *potager*, no more than fifteen feet by fifteen, Paul and Heather grow herbs and salad plants, some fruit and a few vegetables. Beds full of thyme and onions edged with lettuces and box, and other beds with sorrel and dwarf beans, and chives and mint, carrots with yet more onions (not there to ward off the carrot fly, as I thought, but because onions are much relished in the house), are all arranged around a circular bed whose shape is echoed by the head of a standard gooseberry four feet up in the air. The enclosing walls and trellis support espaliered apples, and are entwined with sweet peas and honeysuckle.

I mention elsewhere a particular dark crimson, almost dusky maroon, penstemon, and I was fortunate enough to be given cuttings by Paul Williams. It grows in a large clump near the conservatory on the south-east corner of Bourton House. Called 'Blackbird', it was

On the west side, Bourton House

entrusted to Paul by Ron Sidwell who raised this desirable variety at his home under Bredon Hill a few miles away. I am assured it is bone-hardy.

All around the garden at Bourton House, on terraces, in the courtyards, along paths, and even in the borders, there are pots, pots spilling over with geraniums and summer-flowering perennials and sometimes annuals, pots with foliage plants and succulents. It must be a watering nightmare, but not one single tub or trough looked remotely hard-done-by last summer, and that was a season by which to judge well and truly the success of container gardening.

Again and again on our seemingly endless trundles around Cotswold gardens Simon Dorrell and I were brought up short by the stunning simplicity of one or another little bit of understated planting, well able to compete for effect with the grandest of schemes. It happened again at Bourton House: a low drystone wall made of random Cotswold stone running beside a pathway leading to the magnificent long barn (dated 1570) has, at its base, falling a little over the gravel, a single row of lavender. Just that. Nothing else. One might almost ask, why garden?

MR AND MRS DAVID PEAKE

SEZINCOTE

Near Moreton-in-Marsh, Gloucestershire

Imagine strolling through unspoilt English countryside, by a quiet river under a forest of oaks. It is late spring or early summer; dawn mist prevents distant views and the sounds of nature buzz, caw and chirrup in your ears. The blue and cinnamon arrow of a kingfisher's darting flight pierces your concentration and causes you to raise your eyes. Above, an emerging sun, sailing over emerald banks, reveals a curious turquoise shape. Has your retina held the bird's exotic pigment? Have your far-away thoughts momentarily transferred you to another continent? Is it a mirage?

Equally bizarre would be your orthodox and correct approach to the house:

> Oxford May mornings! When the prunus bloomed
> We'd drive to Sunday lunch at Sezincote:
> First steps in learning how to be a guest,
> First wood-smoke-scented luxury of life
> In the large ambience of a country house.
> Heavy with hawthorn scent were Cotswold lanes,
> Golden the church towers standing in the sun,
> And Gordon Russell with his arts and crafts
> Somewhere beyond in Broadway. Down the drive,
> Under the early yellow leaves of oaks;
> One lodge is Tudor, one in Indian Style.
> The bridge, the waterfall, the Temple Pool –
> And there they burst on us, the onion domes,
> *Chajjahs* and *chattris* made of amber stone:
> 'Home of the Oaks,' exotic Sezincote!

Stately and strange it stood, the Nabob's house,
Indian without and coolest Greek within,
Looking from Gloucestershire to Oxfordshire:
And, by supremest landscape-gardener's art,
The lake below the eastward slope of grass
Was made to seem a mighty river-reach
Curving along to Chipping Norton's hills.

That was Sir John Betjeman recalling his youthful days as an undergraduate in the 1920s in his long autobiographical poem, *Summoned By Bells*, in which he gives several interesting glimpses of the garden at that time, and writes a colourful sketch of the Dugdales who lived there until a year or so before Sir Cyril and Lady Kleinwort acquired the estate in 1944. Many years later the Poet Laureate returned, bearing a bunch of three freesias, when the BBC were making a film to mark his eightieth birthday. But Sir John was not the first to publish impressions of this extraordinary place. Humphry Repton, writing his Red Book, *Designs for the Pavillion at Brighton* (1808), said '. . . a little before my first visit to Brighton, I had been consulted by the proprietor of Sesincot, in Gloucestershire, where he wished to introduce the Gardening and Architecture which he had seen in India.' Repton had been considered as possible architect for the Prince Regent's commission to build the Brighton Pavilion, but that 'privilege' was eventually handed to John Nash eleven years later.

Sezincote was built for Charles Cockerell (Member of Parliament for Evesham) who retired from the East India Company in 1805 and achieved a baronetcy in 1809. He had inherited the estate from his brother, Colonel John Cockerell, who died in 1798. The house was designed by yet another brother, Samuel Pepys Cockerell (also architect of nearby Daylesford House), and the artist Thomas Daniell, both of whom had spent a period in northern India. All these Cockerells were grandsons of John Jackson, nephew of the diarist Samuel Pepys.

The building is 'a mixture of Hindu and Muslim detail which makes [it] a unique example of the architecture of Akbar . . . best known of the Moghuls, ruling from 1556 to 1605'. It stands today much as it first appeared. The 'amber stone' was quarried just a few miles away at

Bourton-on-the-Hill, and some sources attribute its rich colour to a staining process.

Curving in an arc on the south side of the house is the Orangery, forming a quarter of a circle. Here Sir Cyril and Lady Kleinwort (Mrs Peake's parents) laid out the South Garden in 1968 'with canals and rows of Irish yews, copying the traditional Paradise Garden much used by Babur (the first Moghul)'. They were assisted in the planting of this area by Graham Stuart Thomas, whose little pamphlet pointing out many of the plants in the garden is available to today's visitors.

The landscaped garden is of an earlier vintage, with mature cedars of Lebanon now approaching two hundred years old. Entering today, as visitors have for almost two centuries, we walk down the drive and cross the bridge decorated with lotus flowers and four recumbent Brahmin bulls. The bridge straddles a ravine where water flows from the pond beneath the Temple to Surya (the Hindu sun god) in that part of the garden known as the Thornery. There is a pale planting scheme around the clear spring-fed water in the pool, composed of silver-margined *Aralia elata* 'Variegata', white mop-head hydrangeas, a tumbling honeysuckle with greyish leaves (*Lonicera korolkowii*) with ground-covering *Geranium macrorrhizum* and *Buddleia alternifolia* for magenta and pale mauve seasonal contrast. Towering above this grouping is a yew tree reaching some sixty feet or so. In its branches and hanging down in generous swags are *Rosa filipes* 'Kiftsgate' and 'Paul's Himalayan Musk', planted by Lady Kleinwort. Their curtains of bloom in summer light up the yew, causing visitors frequently to ask what the curious 'flowering tree' is.

There are many unusual and some rare trees at Sezincote, some planted by today's owners, some dating from previous generations of occupants. As the water from the Temple pool takes it course down the garden, flowing under the bridge to the string of remaining pools, it passes near Nootka cypress (from western North America), honey locust (*Gleditsia triacanthos* 'Sunburst'), *Acer pensylvanicum*, weeping white mulberry and *Ginkgo biloba*. Another special tree found in this part of the garden is *Rhus potaninii*, a sumach with handsome foliage and reliably rich autumn colour, and producing suckers which enable more of its kind to be planted out elsewhere at Sezincote.

None of the trees just mentioned is native to this country (although

The Temple dedicated to Surya, Sezincote

the mulberry was introduced centuries ago to encourage the silk industry) but most of them now sit contentedly in the British landscape, recognisable as aliens only to dendrologists and the most knowledgeable of gardeners. Some, of course, still manage to look as if they have dragged their anchor to an unlikely shore. In this country we are used to seeing palms in Cornish gardens; here in the north Cotswolds they seem at odds with the landscape, until one turns and is reminded of the spectacular orient-influenced architecture. *Trachycarpus fortunei*, the Chusan palm, named for Robert Fortune who 'introduced' it into Britain in 1849 (but *first* brought to this country by Philip von Siebold nineteen years earlier) actually comes from China; from distant South America but equally at home is the Chilean bamboo, *Chusquea couleou*. Another bamboo, *Arundinaria nitida* from China whose canes can reach ten feet or more, makes impenetrable circular clumps which have to be constantly restrained to prevent unwanted invasion.

Masses of perennial plants have settled themselves in the beds which meander beside the stream on its journey through the pools to the River Evenlode and, eventually, the Thames. *Veratrum album*, hostas, *Lysichitum americanum* (skunk cabbages), white bleeding hearts, peonies and *Peltiphyllum peltatum* (a large member of the saxifrage family, now irritatingly renamed *Darmera peltata*) crowd the banks in the warmer months adding a streamside froth that appears to widen the banks.

Passing under the bridge on stepping stones, with the Brahmin bulls lying on the balustrading above, we are faced with the tall three-headed Snake Fountain which spouts water drawn from its own pool. It entwines itself around an old tree stump standing on its own small island thickly planted with Chinese cowslips (*Primula florindae*) which flower in late spring. On the limestone Cotswold water goes, irrigating ever more trees and shrubs whose ancestry is recorded thousands of miles away. The origins of some can be read in their Latin names: *Mahonia japonica* and *Cornus kousa chinensis* are self-explanatory examples, but most people would need to consult the manuals to discover that *Hydrangea involucrata* comes also from Japan (and Taiwan), and that a garden familiar like *Viburnum davidii*, with steely, turquoise berries in autumn, was introduced to British gardens from the remote hills of western China.

Beside an outcrop of rock another pool collects and holds the water. Again, in boggy beds shaped to follow the water's course, more bold groups of herbaceous plants add a natural element. Astilbes, smilacina and arums enjoy the moist conditions, and bronze sheaves of phormiums make exciting and convincing contrast. The last pool, to be crossed by a planked bridge with a platform over the water, is surrounded with royal ferns and native flag irises. A pocket of naturally-occurring acid loam exists in the predominantly alkaline soil, and this has allowed a grove of rhododendrons to survive. Oddly enough, these appear more alien in a Cotswold limestone garden than many of the exotics from around the temperate world.

In the Orangery there are less-hardy plants from warmer parts of the planet that need to be helped through long English winters with the protection of glass and possibly some gentle heat in severe times. Cassias, jasmines, fremontodendrons, plumbagos, abutilons and *Cestrum* 'Newellii' with large orange-red flowers, tucked up well in this great arc of glass, would all most likely be sent to early graves if left outside through the winter. The dubiously-hardy double form of *Rosa banksiae* 'Lutea' flowers freely indoors, and although it seems to flourish on an exposed terrace at Powis Castle on the Welsh border, it is probably not tough enough to withstand a hard wintery spell in the Cotswolds. Growing up each of the pillars in the Orangery is *Trachelospermum jasminoides*, and planted in beds in alternate bays are purple-leaved heucheras and fuchsias. The doors of the Orangery are left open in summer and this ventilation is vital to good plant health. The Orangery terminates elegantly in an octagon, and it is here that tubs of New Zealand cabbage (*Cordyline australis*) and other tender plants from the garden are over-wintered.

The word Sezincote has evolved from Cheisnecote, which is how the site is recorded in the Domesday Book. It means 'the hillside of the oaks'. Mr and Mrs Peake are aware of the need to continually examine their trees and replace specimens, not only for the sake of the estate and its future owners or custodians, but for the benefit of the countryside as a whole. Appropriately the trees from which the name comes are not neglected, and many saplings have recently been planted to ensure that the famous hillside remains clad with mighty oaks for generations to come.

THE OLD POST OFFICE

Chastleton, Oxfordshire

The entrance to Penelope Mortimer's cottage, in a deeply-cut lane under the mighty walls of Chastleton House, is marked by a George V postbox set in a traditional brick pillar. As a reminder of the days when half this building was a working post office, letters are still collected twice a day. A white-painted wicket gate and low hooped railings define the front area, planted in the best cottage-garden style: tall campanulas, lavender and lax roses wriggling through a border leading straight to the front door. To the right a taller gate in a high fence admits garden visitors to the three-quarters of an acre which Mrs Mortimer has made into a garden of unusual appeal, and which she continues to fine-tune.

Very few gardeners 'get it right' first time round and, besides, most people's ambitions and desires change as they go along. What thrills one year, may pall the next; and gardeners everywhere must learn which plants suit not only themselves, but their soil and climate too. Mrs Mortimer has made many changes to her original plan. Not long ago a box-edged kitchen garden in the *potager* style gave way to today's small formal rose garden, and a large island bed occupying a great part of the sloping site has been transformed as a result of an experience which the owner had while working in Kent two years ago.

But go back to the high gate, which is where a tour begins. It opens into the Red Border, over which there is a view to the Lawn Border, well-designed to cradle that part of the garden which occupies the lowest ground. Like a comforting arm it holds a sufficiently strong planting scheme to prevent the eye from running out of the garden and back across the lane.

Alliums in the Purple Border, The Old Post Office

There are roses everywhere. Mrs Mortimer has referred to them as her 'rose library', and their number includes many distinguished old favourites like 'Fantin Latour', 'Quatre Saisons', 'Louise Odier' and 'Tuscany Superb'. Among these venerable names can be found the newcomers 'Heritage', 'Pretty Jessica', 'Perdita' and 'Chaucer', all from David Austin's 'New English Rose' stable.

Above the terrace, behind the cottage, the land rises gently and the higher you stroll the more relaxed the planting becomes. Large shrubs and small trees are knitting together to form a copse in which on hot summer days it is possible to recline, and look back through leaves to an array of flowers in their allotted beds below.

Beautifully hidden among surrounding branches is a powerful life-size statue, 'Father and Son', made of resin-bronze by the sculptor Philip Hough. It depicts a naked man lifting a baby, with all the love and care in the world. It is the sort of piece enhanced greatly by being discovered in the boscage – its tenderness and human passion would be lost if it were sited on a sunlit terrace, exposed crudely under the bright light of day.

Just a few paces from this statue there begins the long, new, Purple Border whose idea was carried back from Kent in 1989. During the summer of that year Penelope Mortimer, who had written the screenplay for the television production of Nigel Nicolson's *Portrait of a Marriage*, spent several days with the film crew at Sissinghurst Castle. She returned to the Cotswolds having been 'overwhelmed' by Vita Sackville-West's Purple Border, and set about creating for herself something containing the same spirit. An existing 'fairly narrow border of old roses' was quadrupled in width and a frantic search begun to acquire the 'Sissinghurst plants', some of which were hard to find.

At Sissinghurst Castle the Purple Border is backed by a long, high brick wall; no such feature was available here but, within twelve months, a curious similarity to the original has been achieved. Fortunately the planting at Sissinghurst Castle is well labelled so Mrs Mortimer was easily able to draw up her shopping list. She would need, besides the noted roses and clematises, the phlox 'Cool of Evening', *Baptisia australis*, *Melianthus major*, *Knautia macedonica*, dark penstemons including Vita's treasured 'Sour Grapes', and half a

Father and child amongst the trees, The Old Post Office

dozen campanulas. Asters and Japanese anemones and the 'Emperor of China' chrysanthemum would be required to prolong the season.

Mrs Mortimer provides a list of the plants she has successfully tracked down and planted. It is open to speculation how many of these Vita herself would have known, and how many have been added to the famous border by the National Trust's gardeners since she died in 1962. But that is not the point. What matters is the journey, so to speak, not the arrival. It is certain that Mrs Mortimer's border *is* close in spirit to what the Nicolsons were attempting, and it has worked far more convincingly than the countless disappointing imitations of Sissinghurst Castle's White Garden encountered around the temperate world. Let us hope that Penelope Mortimer doesn't abandon this scheme too soon, for it adds a grand effect to a cottage garden miles from the distant corner of England whence its inspiration is derived.

THE HON. PETER AND MRS WARD

CORNWELL MANOR

Cornwell, Oxfordshire

Cornwell Manor, built mainly around 1640 during a difficult moment in England's history, stands above the Evenlode Valley with three north Cotswold towns (Moreton-in-Marsh, Chipping Norton and Stow-in-the-Wold) set in a triangle about it. The village (mentioned in the Domesday Book) is embraced in common ownership with Manor, church, village houses, farms and acreage. Old as the fabric of these buildings is, the story of Cornwell Manor's gardens as they are today begins centuries later.

Like Lawrence Johnston's mother thirty years before her, Mrs Anthony Gillson was another American in search of an English country estate. It was she who, in an attempt to prevent it becoming a 'derelict hamlet', engaged the great Welsh architect Clough Williams-Ellis to work on buildings and grounds. Sir Clough Williams-Ellis (1883–1978) had by then already begun his most famous contribution to British architecture, Portmeirion on the west coast of Wales, and was earning for himself a fine reputation, though he never achieved the status of his near-contemporary, Sir Edwin Lutyens.

In addition to the attention he gave the buildings, Williams-Ellis also worked on the stream which runs through the village and along the lowest level of the Manor garden. He made a formal canal interrupted by a shallow lozenge-shaped pool which, to this day, beautifully reflects the dignified façade of the house above. Willows and *Acer griseum* overhang the edges of the pool and in autumn their leaves float away with those from a small avenue of *Pyrus salicifolia* 'Pendula' lining the easternmost arm of the canal. David Hatchett, Head Gardener since 1976, is convinced that this is the only way to

A view from the formal pool, Cornwell Manor

grow this now so-fashionable tree, and he was able to point out elsewhere in the garden its improved effect when planted in pairs.

The terrace on the south side of the house is wide and functional. Its gravel surface, harrowed weekly to rid it of weeds in the growing season, provides a unique 'breathing space' before the plunge into the horticultural glories of the five-acre ornamental garden. The present owner, the Hon. Peter Ward, has undertaken extensive planting since he acquired the estate in 1959.

The most imposing part of Cornwell Manor is its east-facing terrace punctuated by six tightly clipped Portugal laurels growing in rectangular box-edged beds. From here there is a typically English view encompassing garden, stream and lakes, and rolling Cotswold farmland. Standard wisterias close to the house, but not supported by it, are martyrs to the high winds which can slash suddenly through these upland wolds, though on still days in late summer the harshest intrusion is likely to be the regular snipping noise of hand-shears busy on the topiary and low hedges.

'The Fiddler', a tall, merry piece of sculpture on a central plinth, marks a crossing point on the terrace from which a path can be taken to the Spring Garden whose grassed 'floor' early in the year is successively blue with scillas, then gold with daffodils. Ornamental cherries are planted on a widely-spaced grid and the rise in level at the entrance is marked by the first example of a pair of weeping willow-leaved silver pears. The other exceptional example is situated in the secluded Maid's Garden, a small walled enclosure tucked away but near the house where the two pears, in all their proper raggedness, stand sentinel-like over a calm lawn and richly-planted borders beside the shade of a mulberry tree.

A long lavender hedge acts like a cuff to a bulging assortment of shrubs and climbers on the front of the house. More lavender, and alstroemeria, make neat embellishments under balustrading and beside paths leaving the terrace. From here it is possible to stroll down the grass banks to the lower water garden, or for a more formal departure a flight of stone steps descends to the reflecting pool which holds the 'Boy and Serpents' statue.

Along the stream's banks gunneras have increased in number. Happy with their feet in water they slurp ever onwards to the first lake. In springtime there is a rush of waterside colour from vast colonies of native flag iris (*Iris pseudacorus*), varieties of Siberian irises, mimulus and water mint. This picture is further enriched when marsh marigolds enter the scene together with lavender drumstick primulas, stately Himalayan cowslips and other primula species and hybrids in shades of orange and red.

Rare and unusual trees are planted throughout this landscape; *Magnolia obovata* (syn. *M. hypoleuca*, introduced from Japan in the mid-1800s) gives freely in June of its creamy-white fragrant flowers, eight inches across. *Parrotia persica* from the Caucasus and northern Iran, and *Catalpa bignonioides*, are two further examples of hardy exotica flourishing here in 'middle England'.

As he climbs back towards the house, a visitor's eyes can be forgiven for straying towards a delightful muddle of outbuildings and cottages, including a handsome four-square dovecot. Be taken by your eyes, and follow on to discover further enclosed gardens, large and small. An upward sloping path directs you to the Pool Garden where, with great discretion, a sheet of the brightest turquoise water lies hidden below eye-level so as not to intrude upon the view of the summer-house tucked into the corner of high walls. On the left-hand side and below pool level, like the segments of a great cut grapefruit, there are triangular beds containing (in the summer of 1990) some dramatic yet essentially simple plantings. One segment, for instance, edged in dark 'Hidcote' lavender, was filled with *Achillea* 'Moonshine' whose clear

A view of the Water Garden, Cornwell Manor

On the East Terrace, Cornwell Manor

pale yellow flower heads are vastly superior to the more-often planted
'Cloth of Gold': the fierce yolky yellow of this can, at a stroke, ruin a
subtle scheme. Another of these satisfactory groups includes a
massing of lime green tobacco plants, while another glows with the
stained-glass-window reds of ruby and garnet penstemons.

The long wall bounding this garden has, at its foot, a narrow border
planted thickly with peonies and flowering shrubs and climbers,
relishing every scrap of warmth and protection from the wall. The
Moroccan broom, *Cytisus battandieri,* with its yellow flowers, has pushed
its head above the top of the wall and will probably suffer accordingly
from a wintery onslaught, but it will always respond to spring pruning
and unless the frosts have been severe enough to penetrate between
its toes it will bounce back and give generously of its tinned-pineapple
fragrance the following summer. Honeysuckles and cluster roses share
this fortunate micro-climate and provide a well-scented curtain
through which a path leads to the Vegetable Garden.

This kitchen garden of one and a quarter acres is walled on three
sides leaving the southern aspect open to more benign meteorological
influences. The gently-sloping ground has been worked for over two
hundred years. A central east–west avenue of Cox's Orange Pippin

and Bramley Seedling is flanked by large rectangular beds utilised and rested in alternate years in thoughtful consideration of their ability to continue supplying the Manor with ample produce. Against the walls fan-trained plums, gages and pears enjoy the very best of accommodation overlooking a scene of year-round activity. A yardful of essential buildings includes a boiler-house, propagating house and frames, tomato house, pot store, tool shed and office. And right beside these sits David Hatchett's Jacobean cottage, from which he can keep his thumb on the pulse of this horticultural empire.

David's wife Julie, who used to work for the famous Cotswold alpine plantsman Joe Elliott at his nursery not far away, continues to exercise her skill in raising unusual plants, to sell on the few occasions in the year when Cornwell Manor opens its gates to allow visitors a glimpse of its immaculately-kept and well-fashioned garden.

INTERLUDE

I

Sudeley Castle – Winchcombe, Gloucestershire
The Old Rectory – Great Rollright, Oxfordshire
Swinbrook House – Swinbrook, Oxfordshire
Sherborne House – Sherborne, Gloucestershire
A Cottage in the Windrush Valley, Gloucestershire
Greyhounds – Burford, Oxfordshire

This Interlude – devised, like its three companions, to reveal glimpses of other gardens in addition to those occupying whole chapters – takes us across a great sweep of Cotswold country bringing together six gardens which could hardly be exceeded in their diversity.

Near Winchcombe, the magnificence of SUDELEY CASTLE is today mirrored by the splendour of its formal gardens. The ruins have been threaded with climbing roses, indicating to us how parts of Kiftsgate Court might look if Diany Binny's dreams of removing her roof had ever come true.

Buildings on the present site of Sudeley date from the turn of the thirteenth and fourteenth centuries. Its past owners have included Richard III, Henry VIII's last queen, Catherine Parr and, much later, the glove manufacturing family of Dent. Jane Fearnley-Whittingstall, author of a book about rose gardens, has been working for the past five years with today's owner, Lady Ashcombe, and the gardens are now inbued with a look of graceful order.

Their noble architectural tracery still intact and high trees around them, the glorious old ruins make the perfect home for roses to romp and ramble. Now Climbing 'Lady Hillingdon' is among the roses which lace the inner walls of the ruined castle like great swags of curtain and her soft, apricot-coloured petals perfectly complement the weathered stone. 'Lady Hillingdon' has a marked fragrance, reminiscent of China tea.

Outside, on land with far-reaching views of the sheep-grazed wold, there is a large formal garden whose paths are made of gravel and of grass. Stone balustrading surrounds a central pond, and if your visit coincides with a day when the coachloads have not come, you will be hypnotised by the peace, the grandeur, and the sweet-smelling scents which issue from the herbs and roses. The central beds in each quadrant have a mounded effect created by the way in which the dividing spokes and segments are clipped up to the bowls of urns standing on pedestals. Edgings of sage, cotton-lavender, hyssop and germander define the pattern of beds. Standard-grown roses are important elements of the design; they are repeated throughout the intricate scheme and consist of species and cultivars. 'New Dawn', 'Félicité et Perpétue' and 'Albéric Barbier' are among the better-known examples here, while the recently-found 'Abandonata' is still relatively unknown. More, low-growing, roses are planted among the herbs and aromatics as a part of the overall design. This series of formal beds is

The Queen's Garden, Sudeley Castle

Quatrefoil, Sudeley Castle

surrounded by a wide yet low evergreen hedge, with domes of golden yew in the corners.

Sudeley Castle garden has many surprises; there are broad walks, and secret places. Near the exit leading to the remarkably comprehensive plant-sales area there is a place known as The Mulberry Garden. Branches from the old tree whose name it takes have touched the ground and rooted in one or two places. They provide perfect shady conditions for an underplanting of hellebores, crown imperials, peonies, day lilies and hostas.

In 1989 Jane Fearnley-Whittingstall recreated a little piece of Sudeley's extraordinary atmosphere in London when she made a display with old roses and bits of masonry at the Chelsea Flower Show. It was for many visitors the outstanding exhibit that year, and one that took me off to Sudeley at a hare's pace. Fortunately the real thing extends far beyond a few square yards of exhibition space, and it *is* permanent.

Leaping now to the north Cotswolds, into Oxfordshire, we call at Mr Michael and Lady Joanna Stourton's garden at Great Rollright.

The entrance courtyard at THE OLD RECTORY is finished in gravel, and by the gate there is a cameo of exquisite planting made up of quite ordinary plants, not rarities, but most beautifully put together.

Verbascum in the Mixed Border at The Old Rectory

In the small formal garden at The Old Rectory

It consists of one tree peony, a white rose, some achillea and a few pulmonarias, with silver-leaved stachys, alchemilla and some catmint lying over the sand-coloured stones: it presented us with one of the highlights of our summer garden visiting.

The main part of this garden descends a gentle hillside, but around the house there has been some clever use made of yew hedging to mask one small section from another. It all began twenty years ago and today it is a restful, private garden seeming happily not to concern itself with any of the hectic, high-power horticultural competitiveness which appears to go on everywhere, not just around the Cotswolds.

There are natural-looking ponds at the lowest level, for diving into and swimming in on hot days, approached by a shady walk constructed of flowering shrubs and springtime bulbs. A group of cricket-bat willows enjoys the damp conditions around the pond, and one of them has been decorated with the white-flowering 'Bobbie James', a climbing rose named for the late Hon. Robert James whose garden, St Nicholas, at Richmond in Yorkshire – still open to the public – is thought to have influenced Lawrence Johnston and been an inspiration to him when he was making his own garden at Hidcote Manor.

For me the thrill of visiting The Old Rectory was to discover the small formal knot garden with its gravel paths and box-edged beds. The centre shape is oval, paved in herring-bone-laid bricks carrying a rustic-looking stone plinth surmounted by the figure of a child. The bars and straps of the knot are made of variegated box and teucrium. The beds they form are filled with an assortment of herbs and aromatic plants including thymes, white lavender and santolina. A standard-grown 'Little White Pet' rose rises from each of the beds, and on the outside evergreen 'walls', little pyramids and balls of box have been shaped out of the hedging at regularly-spaced intervals. A fern-leaf metal bench sits at one end, and on a warm spring or summer day this must be the perfect place to hide with a book, or, as in our case, with cones of vanilla ice which had been brought from over the hill.

Travelling south from these hills towards Burford we cross the Evenlode valley and climb once more to high ground, with spectacular views over our shoulder. As the narrow lane begins its long descent to the village of Swinbrook on the banks of the River Windrush, we stop to appreciate the little-known garden of SWINBROOK HOUSE, the home of Mr and Mrs J. D. MacKinnon.

At the heart of this large, modern agricultural estate lies a hidden garden where it is possible to forget the pressures of late twentieth-century life, aided perhaps by the intoxicating scents and colours of full-blown herbaceous borders and mounds of shrub roses.

Statues of two snarling Chinese dogs sitting on a wall each side of stone steps belie the restful atmosphere generated by hundreds of closely-planted perennial plants in a range of soft colours. While the

Lilies and campanula, Swinbrook House

On approaching the garden, Swinbrook House

overall effect is one of blurred harmony there are individual moments of stunning plantsmanship which become prominent on close inspection. Tall white lilies have timed the production of their scented trumpets to coincide with equally tall campanulas ringing their pale blue bells. Hostas cover the ground below them. Irises and bergenias and more hostas bring the borders to life early in the year, and later there will be the acid yellow of alchemilla to set off blue delphiniums, catmint and the blue thistle-like echinops. *Corydalis lutea* spills from the dry cracks in the wall and its bright shade of yellow associates well with the bluey patina of the oriental canines fashioned in lead.

Silvery tones come from several *Pyrus salicifolia* 'Pendula' whose branches have been left to trail the ground. Together with purple-leaved berberis they help to obscure the drystone walls that make a prison of the world beyond.

Sherborne village lies to the north of the A40 Oxford-to-Cheltenham road. SHERBORNE HOUSE partly dates from the sixteenth century but was largely 'rebuilt' between 1829 and 1834, and has recently been remodelled into apartments. However, it still closely resembles the mansion as it appeared in an engraving published in 1712. The parish church of St Mary Magdalene sits next to the house and enjoys the same parkland setting.

Among the many elements to please a garden visitor at Sherborne is
the large, seven-bay orangery or conservatory. Its high sash windows –
almost floor to ceiling – are reflected in the surface water of a large
rectangular, raised pond, which during a period of the house's
previous life as a school was a swimming pool built by pupil labour.
Today there are water-lilies, irises and ornamental grasses, and on a
very hot day last year this brimming pool appeared as an oasis among
desert-coloured lawns burnt by that summer's drought.

Refreshed by the calm and cooling influences of the still water, we
wandered into the parkland's shade to discover a classical gazebo
whose parapet is supported by two elegant columns. It is possible to
sit here and reflect on the rolling countryside – a perfect antidote to
the bedding-out of annuals whose vivid flowers greet visitors at the
main entrance to the house. This display is an acknowledgement of
Victorian taste and a tribute to the gardeners who slave for its
perfection.

There is an inner courtyard, too, with shady and cool cloisters to
walk in on hot summer days. Hanging baskets with bright geraniums
tumbling from them have been placed in each stone arch, and this
suburban embellishment manages somehow to create a pleasing, if
somewhat curious, effect.

In the cloisters, Sherborne Park

A cottage garden in the Windrush Valley

On another day we travelled along the VALLEY of WINDRUSH in late afternoon on our way to see the Parkers' garden at Minster Lovell. In many ways there are prettier and more typical-looking Cotswold villages and hamlets, and we would not pretend for a moment that Windrush makes any special claims. We were stopped in our tracks, though, by the sight of a cottage which in every detail seemed the archetypal 'picture book' country dwelling.

The ground-floor windows look out through draping honeysuckles and clematis. The stone path, leading straight to the oak front door, is lined with lavender so thickly planted that you feel you should approach sideways. Roses are everywhere, pink roses mostly, falling over the boundary wall and leaning over the neighbours' fence; poppies and hollyhocks sway in the breeze. We could only imagine how the back garden might look.

We asked in the village when the occupants might be home. No one
knew. They were weekenders, we were told; no one seemed to know
their name. We called again on another day, but still no reply came in
answer to our knock. We could have left a message in the letter-box.
Instead we just stood again to admire the vision of this uniquely
English scene. And then we drove away, feeling better for having
shared at least a few moments in this garden's life while its owners,
probably, were otherwise engaged in Birmingham, Bristol or London.
How they must have longed for Windrush.

Not far from Windrush is Burford, and GREYHOUNDS is the famous
address in Sheep Street of the little magazine in green covers which
has been delighting bands of country-minded readers for several
generations.

The Countryman was founded in 1927. Its circulation continues to
grow, and its surprisingly large garden, reached through a covered
way and by a flight of wide stone steps, is open on any day of the week
for its readers to visit. Today's editor is only the fourth in a direct line
from the man who started the whole thing. Christopher Hall enjoys
the garden, and like me when I am wearing my own editorial cap, he

On approaching the garden at Greyhounds

takes proofs and typescripts to a favourite seat on those warm days when the wind isn't too playful. The idea of doing some office work in the garden is very appealing, and who would not exchange the tyranny of the telephone for the peaceful, dappled shade of an ancient mulberry.

The Countryman has earned for itself a niche in English horticulture by having a new rose named in its honour, bred by David Austin in 1987 to commemorate the sixtieth anniversary of the magazine's life. In his book *The Heritage of the Rose* David Austin describes the flowers of 'The Countryman' as 'quite large, loosely double rosettes, deep pink in colour, with an exceptional Old Rose fragrance'. He goes on to say that they have something of the spirit of the peonies we see in Chinese and Japanese paintings. The specimens in *The Countryman*'s garden are still small; I hope they come up to full expectation, and if the rose lasts in cultivation for as long as the sturdy little magazine whose name it carries, it should have a bright future.

Greyhounds at Greyhounds

MANOR FARM

Minster Lovell, Oxfordshire

'No pleached limes for me.' Thus Jill Parker, commenting on the making of the garden that spreads itself near the banks of the River Windrush where pollarded and broken willows, scattered among the water meadows, comprise the quintessentially English idyll. Minster Lovell Hall, a ruin since the middle of the eighteenth century, dominates the scene.

Sir Peter and Lady Parker lead full lives, although Lady Parker has recently retired from her National Health general practice. They acquired the rambling run-down farmhouse and its treasury of fine old stone barns in the autumn of 1973. At around that time I was spending many weekends at Oxford, and I remember being taken to see the ruined Hall on a bright but cold winter morning. The vision of the circular dovecot has remained in my mind, and I remember thinking then how splendid it would look in a garden setting: it does.

Having openly declared her own version of paradise – '. . . old-fashioned roses falling out of apple trees. Dappled grass and secret places. Sentimental as you please . . .' – Lady Parker rushed headlong into a frenzy of planting.

Her garden site had for its backdrop all the romance she needed to be getting on with. She has been undaunted by some of the stoniest possible ground, and has transformed the gently sloping terrain to a voluptuous, seemingly carefree abundance of roses, clematis, herbs and summer flowers which thread themselves hither and thither around the medley of cart-houses, barns, hay-stores and a three-seat communal privy, now reborn as the sweeter-smelling Summer-house.

Lady Parker has achieved many of her goals in a remarkably few years, in reality a shorter time still when you consider it has been mostly a weekend labour. Her sister Pat has been an indispensable guide and mentor, and now that she has moved from Kent to Burford she will be on hand to help even more.

'The Garden part of the garden', as Jill Parker calls it, is on the north side of the house, framed majestically from the house by the doorcase that accommodates an unusually wide, iron-studded door. This leads directly on to paving, then cobbles, to grass. Along one of the walls on the shady side of the house is a low hedge of rue, *Ruta graveolens*, whose colour, unadorned by other plants, is a triumph of understatement. The foliage, well-behaved all year long, harmonises perfectly with the yellow-tinged stone, requiring no sunshine to show it off. On the other side of the door the pink climbing rose 'Madame Caroline Testout' intermingles happily with *Hydrangea petiolaris* rising from a colony of hellebores at home in their own damp and sunless corner.

Out in the open, where the sun most certainly falls, some of the inherited apple trees have been allowed to remain. One, 'Beauty of Bath', is now draped with the long white sprays of 'Félicité et Perpétue', a vigorous rambling rose bred in France over one hundred and fifty years ago.

Roses play an important role in this garden and they occupy a warm spot in Lady Parker's heart. Here in midsummer you can encounter species such as *Rosa wichuraiana*, *R. xanthina*, *R. moyesii* and dozens more. Among the famed roses bearing distinguished names familiar to rose lovers everywhere are 'Fantin Latour', 'Constance Spry', 'Buff Beauty', 'Souvenir de la Malmaison', 'Gypsy Boy' and the unromantically labelled, but dreamy, 'Blairi No. 2'. There are infinitely more roses at Manor Farm than I can list here: they do indeed fall out of trees; they flop over walls; they drip from pergolas; and they stand ceremonially in a Rose Circle where once, in years past, a vegetable garden kept the kitchen well supplied.

Clearly the Parkers love jokes and puns. This shows in their naming of parts: Thyme Square ('more thyme than space'); the Golden Gate (an arch planted with the roses 'Highfield' and 'Leverkusen' with *Alchemilla mollis* around their ankles); and the Pearly Gate ('a free-style jumble' where the roses 'Kathleen Harrop', 'Zéphirine Drouhin' and 'Blairi No. 2' fight it out with *Solanum crispum*, the potato vine).

Garden path, Manor Farm

Like my own, the Herb Garden is not hard by the kitchen door, but that matters not. It often makes for a pleasant pre-lunch or early evening stroll to gather the essential flavourings for a simple meal. The Parkers' herb garden, with sundial set on a column in the centre, is in midsummer just the sort of free-for-all that these little patches should be. It always delights me to see the bare bones of a herb garden, particularly a new one or one existing only as a plan on paper, because I know that within weeks of planting all the beautiful, well-reasoned crisp geometry of the thing will have been obscured by the thugs who go by the gentle names of tansy, fennel, soapwort and mint. But that is part of the reason for formal herb gardens, I think. Come winter, we know the bones will resurface.

Even though Jill Parker has made a garden with unlikely or rarely encountered features, she has incorporated a traditional herbaceous border, running along the wall of the woodshed. Strictly speaking it is a mixed border, because it includes roses and other climbers among the more usual campanulas, cranesbills, irises, thalictrums, echinops and peonies.

There are two pools in this garden, neither for family swimming; on my summer visit last year the Parkers' grandchildren were happy to cool themselves with hoses! The pools, or ponds, I refer to are His and Hers, part of the garden's horticultural, not leisure, aspect. They are separated by a low wall which camouflages the two levels, and share the same, recycled, water. Perhaps this is the only example in the garden of two minds, mostly playing the same tune, reading different music. Lady Parker has said that formality is not for her (not in her own garden anyway), but I suspect that Sir Peter (and is this a masculine craving?) enjoys a clean edge, a sharp line and an occasional respite from glorious disarray. Whichever way it is, and I may be quite wrong, each pond would appear to reflect its maker's individual personality. One is natural-looking, set in grass, with reeds and irises at its edge. The other is rimmed with stone, lozenge-shaped and partner to a long pergola for meditating or reading under. Both pieces of water fit well into the scheme of things.

There may be no pool for swimming in, but the family can enjoy tennis or croquet together, and the various parts of the garden are so well-spaced that a feeling of openness is never lost. No one could

The dovecot overlooking the garden at Manor Farm

suffer claustrophobia at Manor Farm garden. No one with an addiction to beautifully planted borders and terraces need suffer withdrawal symptoms, either. And if they do, well, Dr Parker has written
the perfect prescription: her book, *The Purest of Pleasures*, tells the whole
thumping story.

BROADWELL HOUSE

Broadwell, Oxfordshire

W hen I arrived at this garden in January I was apprehensive
about having to make some sort of representation which would
accord with the images Simon Dorrell encountered on his visit in
June. There was one day only during the summer when, for outside
reasons, we were unable see the same gardens together. I am pleased
to be able to say, though, that my midwinter experience was as
rewarding for me as Simon's was for him. By all accounts it was *then* a
question of hurrying from one patch of shade to the next in an attempt
to escape the broiling sun; for me, it was a case of lingering long
enough to appreciate the form of the garden in a cold wind I do not
wish to experience again. Simon had the roses, I had the year's first
snowdrops.

The village of Broadwell suffers bravely the goings-on at nearby
Brize Norton aerodrome, but it is not difficult to imagine the peace
and quiet it once enjoyed before we conquered the air. The village
seems to flow out of its neighbour, Kencot, and is one of a group of
beautiful places lying among water-meadows and level farmland
between Lechlade on the Thames and the high ground which carries
the A40 trunk-road past Burford. Not far away, at Langford, Sir Hardy
Amies has made a fine garden in the grounds of the Old School, and at
Kelmscott, just a few fields distant, Ernest Gimson designed the
Village Hall to commemorate William Morris.

Broadwell House was built in 1720 and sympathetic additions were
made in the 1930s. Charles and Susan Cox came twenty-five years
ago; the garden was laid out in much the same way as we see it now,
but in a quarter of a century of gardening many plants come and go.

Cold spells and storms have taken their toll; in 1982, the Coxes told me, they recorded thirty-nine and a half degrees (Fahrenheit) of frost. This rare dip in the temperature killed a mature cedar of Lebanon. A tall Wellingtonia (*Sequoiadendron giganteum*) still stands, hinting at the atmosphere formerly created by forest trees in a garden setting.

The house lies well back from the road and is surrounded by some seven acres of its own land, although only two of these acres concern us here. This is just the sort of house and garden which trippers and idle motorists will stop to gawp at on a day's outing. The wonderful topiary can be seen from the village street between stone gate-piers; the broad drive leads straight to the house.

The topiary itself predates Brigadier and Mrs Cox's arrival; it is all made of yew and the well-cut shapes seem to imitate cones or sugar-loaves, and form low mounds. They are randomly placed beside a rectangular sunken garden whose edges are of well-weathered stone. The garden has a pale and frothy look in summer with lots of 'The Fairy' rose interplanted with santolina, helichrysum and small-leaved silvery lamiums. Four prostrate junipers with glaucous foliage spread round the corners of the four beds, while a narrow border between the topiary and the walls of the sunken garden is filled with dwarf irises and cheerfully-coloured polyanthus. By the house a new garrya has been planted to replace a previous specimen which became a victim of prolonged winter weather. The white-flowering hebe by the front door seems never to be without flowers, and even on my January day I noticed several brave blooms as Mrs Cox kindly rummaged inside the plant to find me suitable 'soft' cuttings to root. She says this hebe, whose name is lost, strikes easily and she is often able to offer small rooted youngsters for sale on open days. This plant seems to survive the cold very well, and Mrs Cox is using it in her son's garden at Stow-on-the-Wold where, she says, the wind blows straight from Siberia.

Running along the inside of the vine-clad wall by the road is a very wide border, with a stone path edged with a slightly raised, much narrower, border. The main border is bulked up with small trees (*Prunus subhirtella* 'Autumnalis') and large shrubs including choisya, some roses, a seventy-five year old *Acer negundo* 'Variegatum', dark-leaved elder, spiraea, gleditsia, mahonias, euonymus and variegated hollies, all underplanted with a medley of herbaceous flowers and

Tapestry, Broadwell House

great quantities of bulbs. The narrow bed running along the other side of the path has a more delicate-looking range of plants, more appropriate to their ribbon-like bed. Parahebes, rock-roses, pinks, perennial cornflowers and low phloxes hang over the ankle-high wall and spill onto the path. In both these borders, and throughout the whole garden, there are many penstemons which, despite most published warnings, are hardier than we think. One or two had solitary blooms in the first week of the year.

Two semi-circular beds lie beneath the stone wall which forms a right-angle with the main border. One has a yellow theme with 'Allgold' and 'Chinatown' roses, golden elm, 'Bowles' Golden Grass'

(*Milium effusum* 'Aureum'), carex and stipa, with 'Goldheart' ivy falling from the wall above. Its companion bed deals in shades of red with *Carex buchananii* (leatherleaf sedge), reddy-purple-leaved ajugas and bergenias, and the vigorous, frost-hardy fuchsia 'Mrs Popple' whose flowers bring tones of crimson and purple to the scheme.

Behind the well-cut lawn, and surrounded by the borders just described, is a large flat area of rougher grass where specimen trees help to screen neighbouring buildings and provide summer shade. Here will be found a selection of woody plants including many willows, shrub roses, liquidambar, metasequoia, wild cherry, amelanchier, green and variegated aralias, variegated sycamore (*Acer pseudoplatanus* 'Brilliantissimum'), *Caragana arborescens* from the eastern Soviet Union, *Sorbus aria* 'Mitchellii', ginkgo and the American-raised *Cornus* 'Eddie's White Wonder', with large white flowers. The old walnut tree predates the Coxes, and they express some anxiety over its well-being on stormy nights.

The heart of this garden exists near the walls of the house. On the south-facing stone terrace I noticed a 'thatch' of grey-leaved teucrium which had not lost so much as an inch of its reputedly tender stems during the past two clement winters – but as I write, with snow falling all around me, I wonder if it will be lucky for a third year running. (It will shoot again from below ground if the frost destroys its topsail.) Climbing from the terrace onto the house are wisteria, a white banksian rose, pyracantha, *Rosa* 'Mermaid' and several clematis including the evergreen *C. armandii* which displays its snowy-white flowers early in the year.

Still within the heart of Broadwell House's garden there are two ponds – one rectangular, fed via a stone rill by the other, circular, pool which takes its water from a spring that can issue four hundred gallons of water an hour if not regulated. All around the ponds there are low walls and narrow borders, and good trees in wide beds. The well-head is covered in summer with wisteria, and a metal arch is host to the crimson 'Parkdirektor Riggers' rose. Nearby, in winter, is a vivid picture composed of the glowing bark and previous year's twigs on a twenty-foot high *Acer palmatum* 'Senkaki' (the coral bark maple) and the prolific flower clusters of *Viburnum* × *bodnantense* 'Dawn' reaching almost to the same height. There is more fragrance, too, at

Topiary, Broadwell House

the beginning of the year; when I was there the first of the season's yellow wintersweet flowers (*Chimonanthus praecox*) were opening. Later in the year the herbaceous underplanting emerges, and the sight of white honesty under an exochorda with its branches weighed down by chalk-coloured flowers is eagerly awaited.

With my own passion for hellebores, and being aware of how well they grow in this part of the world, I was hoping throughout my amble to discover a bed full of them. I was not disappointed. In a corner, protected by an outbuilding and a wall – beside a thatched summer-house – I found what I yearned for. With evergreen piptanthus behind them, and further billowings of yellow jasmine and tall abutilons, there were the hellebores. Of course I was too early to see them in full flower, but the promise they made guaranteed a return visit at the right moment.

Hard by the house, in a small courtyard forbidden to the worst of the elements, there is a now multi-stemmed arbutus. It was once a large tree but it, too, was a victim of 1982's severe winter weather. As a result a multitude of smaller branches has sprouted from near ground level. Fortunately there is room within the courtyard to accommodate this new figure, and to enliven the remodelled arbutus during the summer, before its strawberry-like fruits appear, Mrs Cox has grown a white potato vine (*Solanum crispum*) through its limbs.

Brigadier and Mrs Cox derive, I think, tremendous pleasure from their garden, and if the enthusiastic and detailed tour which they gave me on a bitterly cold January day is anything to go by, I am only surprised that Simon Dorrell was able to tear himself away from its high-summer splendour.

INTERLUDE

II

The Old Manor – Broadwell, Oxfordshire
Kencot House – Kencot, Oxfordshire
Poulton Manor – Poulton, Gloucestershire
The Little House – Barnsley, Gloucestershire
Yew Tree Cottage – Ampney St Mary,
Gloucestershire
Waterton House – Ampney Crucis,
Gloucestershire
Ewen Manor – Ewen, Gloucestershire

THE OLD MANOR, just a few yards from Broadwell House, was built in 1780. It sits directly opposite the gate to the twelfth- and thirteenth-century church of St Peter and St Paul, and its clipped yews can be seen from the village pavement, even from passing cars; this is gardening in a shop window. Mr and Mrs Chinnery, owners of this house for the past ten years, are luckily very fond of topiary, which makes them perfect guardians of the elegantly-styled evergreens in the front garden; they are, too, creators of new pieces of topiary within their three-quarters of an acre of garden. On the front lawn there is a vase, filled with grey and green hebes, sitting in a circle of box hedge. This scheme looks good all year, and only needs a couple of trailing helichrysums to dress it up for the summer when fear of frost has passed. This small formal area only hints at the way in which the remainder of the garden has been treated, and we have to pass through the high Florentine gate – full of wrought-iron flowers – to penetrate the private world of luxuriant borders and secret places.

The garden beyond the walls, The Old Manor

Reckoning that a high proportion of time is spent in the kitchen, the Chinnerys devised their main pair of flower borders to be enjoyed from this room. Surrounded by *Hydrangea petiolaris*, with hostas in the border below, the kitchen window must be a useful attraction to anyone somewhat shy of fulfilling their share of the domestic duties. These borders are a carnival of colour in summer, brimming with long-flowering plants which include bulbs, herbaceous perennials, roses and shrubs. A very large rugosa rose, 'Roseraie de l'Haÿ', collapsed under 1990's heavy fall of pre-Christmas snow. It will soon shoot many new branches and within another growing season will, I feel sure, reclaim its allotted space. One of the two arches which span the border's path is planted with *Vitis coignetiae* (with good burgundy-coloured leaves in autumn) and white wisteria.

At the far end of the border, on the site of a former vegetable patch, the Chinnerys have made a 'secret' garden room which is entered through four pear trees trained to grow like a section of vaulted ceiling. This quiet space, composed only of hedges and grass, reveals a magical trick: behind the far low hedge, protruding in summer above its clipped top, there is a row of single, white, rugosa roses. This sort of simplicity, an understatement of a powerful kind, never fails to work its spell on me.

Allowing themselves a large lawn within the walls of their garden, Michael and Mardi Chinnery have created a valuable open space with borders all round. On the far side of the garden they have made a 'spring corner' where hellebores, tulips, narcissi, lily-of-the-valley and cyclamen have naturalised contentedly under the reaching arms of an old mulberry. At one end of the lawn Michael Chinnery has planted a neat row of pleached limes. These screen another part of garden, offer some shelter, and impose an architectural element which works as well on a small scale as it does when strung out to define a long vista.

The Chinnerys have one more trick to play: on the other side of the house they have enhanced a small courtyard by laying gravel, placing a pair of conical-shaped box bushes by either side of the door, letting a 'New Dawn' rose infiltrate a wall-trained pear, and allowing a fig to occupy whatever room it needs in exchange for a sure crop of fruit every year. A warm attractive area has thus been made of what might otherwise have become a forgotten corner.

Less than a mile from Broadwell is KENCOT HOUSE, one elegant façade clad in wisteria, *Magnolia grandiflora* and roses. More roses tumble along the garden wall as far as the gate-piers which perfectly frame the pedimented doorcase flanked by Tuscan half-columns. Garden visitors must turn the corner and make an entrance along a broad drive between herbaceous borders.

When Sonia Patrick came to Kencot thirty years ago she found the garden well-furnished with large trees. Two large cedars of Lebanon were killed by frost in 1981. (Who, I wonder, introduced cedars to these villages a hundred years ago?) When Alvilde Lees-Milne lost *her* cedars at Essex House, Badminton early in 1990, she had the stumps routed out of the ground and the space returfed. As Mrs Patrick's trees were not uprooted – they were sawn off above ground – she chose to leave one trunk standing to a height of ten feet or so. This she has curtained with an assortment of five clematis well chosen to display flowers over many months. The first of the group to flower is *Clematis alpina*, in late spring, and the last is *C. orientalis* 'Bill Mackenzie', a variety originating in 1968 at the Waterperry School of Horticulture on the other side of the county.

Frosts have not robbed this garden of all its fine trees; there is a wonderful old weeping silver lime whose sweetly-scented flowers can be enjoyed in the house on days when the windows are open; the ginkgo must be approaching its centenary, and there is a red chestnut of impressive stature. Under the low-spreading limbs of the ginkgo is a springtime cavalcade of aconites, snowdrops, crocuses, fritillaries, hyacinths and small species tulips, whose ragged foliar remains are obscured by the timely emergence of the ginkgo's leaves.

On the lawn surrounded by these trees is a new bed with shrubs and perennials in shades of pink and yellow. In a good season the primroses may be out at the same time as *Lonicera fragrantissima*, with cherry and *Acer negundo* 'Flamingo' coming into flower and leaf a little later. Sonia Patrick collects hardy geraniums, and many of their colours are right for this bed. Alliums and foxgloves spike the foliage of yellow-flowered buddleia and a 'Barnsley' lavatera which, like so many other specimens of this variety I have encountered (including the one in my own garden), is all too quick to produce shoots whose flowers appear to have 'reverted' back to the uninspired purplish-pink shade of the species.

In a wide border by the road, the stump of a second departed cedar has been cut much closer to the ground. Sonia Patrick's response to this one was to plant next to it a spreading juniper whose fan-like branches have now masked the offending relic. A white everlasting pea (*Lathyrus latifolius*) romps adventurously through the juniper.

The level two-acre garden at Kencot House is full of interest; the main lawn is now being planted up with specimen trees at the far end, and the Kitchen Garden – with that great modern-day luxury, grass paths – is a home for traditionally-managed beds of asparagus, leeks,

The garden, from across the drive, Kencot House

Summer-house, Kencot House

peas, beans and all manner of vegetables which are as eagerly sought
by troublesome rabbits as by the owners. The best kitchen gardens in
the world allow themselves some floral decoration; Kencot House is
no exception. Around the ordered beds of edible produce are peony
borders, bulbs for cutting, an orchard, beds of chamomile (for tea),
and a large patch of nasturtiums.

Returning to the house we come across the quartered rose garden.
Some of the roses are now going into a decline, but every attempt is
made to preserve those which can muster a decent appearance or do
not threaten their companions with disease. Tree peonies and many of
Mrs Patrick's treasured penstemons are grown in the Rose Garden,
and in the early months of the year the edges become ribbons of blue
chionodoxas and grape hyacinths. There is a thirteenth-century stone
arch set in the high wall by the Rose Garden, and a vaulted niche
provides what must be one of the most seductive and refreshing
sitting places on a hot summer's day.

Leaving Kencot, travelling through Broadwell to Lechlade, and
following the road through Fairford towards Cirencester, one
passes through a string of Cotswold villages where gardens can
be seen between gates and over hedges. At Poulton it will not be
possible to ignore the handsome house which stands where the
road makes a sharp turn. This is POULTON MANOR, which in its
serenity is the welcome sorbet on a menu of rich, main-course
Cotswold gardens.

Anthony and Erica-Mary Sanford came here in the mid-1960s and although they at once fell in love with and bought the untouched Caroline house, they also became the owners of several acres of neglected and desperate-looking garden. Light was barred from the drawing-room by two tall Irish yews growing unsymmetrically each side of the main door. Despite a craving for air and sunshine, Mrs Sanford could not bear to have them felled. Cranes were brought in, the yews were moved. Today, after some surgery to relieve initial stress, they are essential components of a beautiful garden whose lines are regular, unfussy and thoroughly stimulating.

To two yew hedges found on their arrival the Sanfords have added several more to partition the garden in a theatrical but simple way. Views in and from the garden are strictly controlled. The large lawn is divided by a central path, and running along the wall at the far end is a double row of hornbeams, pleached above bare trunks. The avenue terminates at the south end in a semi-circular apse of hornbeam hedging. This part of the garden, enclosed by walls, appears to be perfectly rectangular – but when it came to making a plan, it was discovered that the walls run off at tangents, deceiving the eye. The correct alignment was achieved by giving the hornbeams a false perspective, so that today there is no worrying geometry.

Mr and Mrs Sanford set up their formal hornbeam allée without any of the recommended intricate framework of rods and rails and special tying-in procedures. After ensuring that the young trees are well staked against gales, the method is to hold the growing tips together with tomato ties when the branches meet, and after the wood has ripened they will remain in the trained position. The density of the pleaching is then controlled by the amount of weaving in and out of the stems, and by cutting others which protrude. The Chinnerys at The Old Manor, Broadwell also discovered this technique for themselves, and both examples of pleaching are precise, properly tailored and an example of how almost everything in the garden can be done by breaking the rules. One can only speculate upon what a fuss modern-day gardening programmes on television would make of all this.

It would be misleading, however, to suggest that everything at Poulton Manor is plain or formal. Mr and Mrs Sanford have borne in

Pleached hornbeams, Poulton Manor

mind that they themselves are the gardeners and if they bite off too much, it will fall only to themselves to maintain order. Gradually, as they have found more time, they have added beds and borders which they are confident of being able to tend properly. A new border now runs the length of the lawn against the six-foot-high stone wall which separates one part of the garden from another. As the wall faces south it was too good to leave unplanted. By fixing almost invisible mesh to the stone, Erica-Mary Sanford has secured a number of roses ('Maiden's Blush', 'Albertine', 'Lady Hillingdon' and 'Céline Fore-stier' – a delicate variety bearing pale yellow, tea-scented flowers, bred in France over one hundred and fifty years ago.) By not making this border too wide Mrs Sanford has kept her future work to a minimum, and by planting large groups of easily-cared-for perennials and sub-shrubs she has insured against a life of toil.

Where the land slopes away from the enclosed lawn a gate in the walls gives access to the meadow where pale narcissi and snake's-head fritillaries crowd around the spring-fed stream which flows away to join the Ampney Brook. This less-manicured area of grass provides sharp and pleasing contrast to the enclosed spaces around the house.

Rose 'The Alchemist', Poulton Manor

There are also various colourful borders at Poulton manor; one is planted for maximum show in spring, another relies for its effect upon the massing together of autumn-flowering cyclamen. Yet another part, by the back of the house, has been designed to give formal pleasure without slavery. It comprises two sets of four beds marked out in variegated box which was increased by cuttings from a few original plants. The design accommodates standard-grown weeping rosemaries in dark-coloured pots, surrounded by beds with marjoram, *Stachys* 'Silver Carpet' and rue.

The finest of all understatements at Poulton Manor appears on the same side of the house as the pattern-garden; without any other touches at all, just one rose, 'The Alchemist', has been given a wall of its own. This is generosity indeed.

Only a few miles away, in the village of Barnsley, Rosemary Verey has been working in a garden across the street from her own celebrated domain. THE LITTLE HOUSE, owned by Arthur and Catharine Reynolds, is protected from the street by a palisade of high, clipped beech. The formal treatment of the narrow 'corridor' between house and road shews another side of Mrs Verey's ability to grace a garden with gestures more usually found around a more imposing building. Here are box balls, standard-grown whitebeams, and geometric beds with the sort of easy-care planting that allows the garden's owners to escape the demands of labour-intensive horticulture. The paving along the front of the house alternates large and small slabs to create a Greek-key effect. Box balls have been placed each side of the smaller pieces and, in a long run, they add strength to the perspective.

Lavenders and 'evergreys' interspersed with low-growing blue and white *Viola cornuta* in the knot garden, with lively fountain splashes behind, make an immediate and stylish impression.

The formal garden, The Little House

The garden at YEW TREE COTTAGE is notable not only for the wide variety of its plants but also for the fact that it has now been open to the public for almost twenty-five years. Mrs Shuker made the garden with her daughter Penny Pollit over the last twenty-eight years.

Gardening begins outside the stone walls where many clematis, love-in-a-mist, roses and irises have been planted. Shrubs and climbers inside have been encouraged to break their bounds.

By the back of the house, a mounded scree bed has been made around a small pond and this adds some height to the otherwise level ground. The wiry stems of *Cotoneaster congesta* spread out over the surrounding gravel and the rocks are now all obscured by spreading armies of alpine plants whose battalions include thymes, dianthus, saxifrages, violas, silenes, cyclamen, erodiums and miniature geraniums.

Both Penny Pollit and her mother are very fond of alpine plants, and grow them in scaled-down gardens converted from old porcelain sinks. In a radio broadcast last year Mrs Pollit gave her 'recipe' for transforming these old kitchen sinks: she dry-mixes one part peat, two parts sand and one part cement, adds water and applies it to the sides of the sink, previously brushed with some form of rubber solution – Unibond, for instance (without this treatment the mixture cannot adhere to the shiny surface). When it is dry she 'paints' on a coat of cow muck

Summer flowers, Yew Tree Cottage

and milk (vital organic ingredients which allow mosses and lichens to grow naturally). The results look like stone-made troughs, and if frost attacks the finish it can be patched up with further dollops of the same stuff. Needless to say there is a large collection of these 'troughs' at Yew Tree Cottage and they contain a wonderful collection of alpines, alas no longer propagated to be offered for sale on open days.

At WATERTON HOUSE the large garden and park was laid out many decades ago and today's owner Gerard Mizrahi is in the process of restoration and further development. The potential exists here to make a fine garden, and I look forward to revisiting Waterton in a few years. There are good trees – copper and cut-leaf beech, a tulip tree and an old robinia among crab apples and flowering cherries – freely distributed about the grounds, and with the spaces which have so far been segmented or defined Mr Mizrahi can hardly go wrong.

Because this is flat country the designer of the garden chose to dig a huge semi-circular ha-ha to prevent an invasion of grazing animals. The ha-ha at Waterton is faced with stone, and it curves right round the house in one vast bay leaving plenty of land within its boundary to make a garden of very good size.

The rose pergola, Waterton House

The rose pergola, laden with red, pink and white climbing roses, is supported by nine pairs of cylindrical columns made of small pieces of Cotswold stone. Although none of the pieces of stone is large, the chunkiest pieces are properly positioned at the base while the thinnest pieces are used towards the top. The pergola spans an eight-foot wide path which leads away from the house to a pair of semi-circular steps and a wooden bridge over the stream. This is an unusual pergola, one which could be easily copied where stone is readily found; what better use for it?

Stone is much in evidence at EWEN MANOR too. The garden dates from just after the Second World War, the house itself was moved from the other side of the River Thames two hundred years earlier. When Colonel and Mrs Gibbs came here in 1947 they found old, overgrown yew hedges, and pieces of lawn reverting to field. Today it ranks as one of the Cotswolds' prize gardens with architectural features and well-planted borders to satisfy the most discerning visitor.

As a child in Scotland, Mrs Gibbs was given a small greenhouse by her father. Having taught herself then how to propagate plants, she has been able to keep this garden well supplied.

Views across the lawn encompass a circular summer-house with Cotswold stone tiles on its conical-shaped roof. There are stone terraces, retaining walls and a pool. Everywhere the planting is profuse – in paving cracks, on the house walls, in long borders, and in open orchard.

One of this garden's distinctive features is the line of eleven golden yews flanking the path by the gently-sloping herbaceous border, which itself is backed by a high green yew hedge. The border consists of mixed planting – herbaceous perennials, roses and shrubs. Behind it, on the other side of the yew, there is a large rectangular lily pond overlooked by a garden room converted from old stables. The pond, with a piece of sculpture by Mrs Gibbs in the centre, is surrounded by masses of yellow, pink and red helianthemums, some alpine phloxes and lots of *Alchemilla mollis* to soften the edges. In midsummer there will be pots of geraniums standing at the corners, and outside the garden room more pots will be filled with myrtle and rosemary.

Path to the pool, Ewen Manor

Steps to the terrace, Ewen Manor

Soon after arriving here, Colonel Gibbs made a large sunken rose garden where potatoes had been grown during the 'Dig for Victory' campaign through the war. Alas the Hybrid Teas deteriorated after a dozen years or so, and rather than spend endless hours spraying and nursing them, Colonel and Mrs Gibbs decided to transform the area to a large grassed garden, with corner beds and a central paved area; today, it appears as a perfect embellishment to the manor house. Fortunately a very large cedar of Lebanon has survived and its presence surveying the sunken garden adds a note of delightful antiquity.

Gardening has been a lifelong pursuit for Mrs Gibbs; at Misarden Park near Stroud her son, Major Wills, carries on the tradition.

LITTLE TULSA

Cecily Hill, Cirencester, Gloucestershire

Within chiming distance of St John the Baptist, Cirencester, the largest parish church in Gloucestershire, Father Beck and his wife have made within their walled plot a garden – strictly speaking, two gardens – which on some open days during the summer months has attracted up to four hundred visitors. The two gardens are His and Hers although, as with everything in a good marriage, there is a sharing of both duties and rewards.

The garden divides into two levels. The smaller 'half', Hers, is situated immediately behind the house through which all visitors must pass. The larger, Father Beck's, is reached by steps to a lower level. They are very different: each visitor must decide for himself whether they reflect the characters of those who work them.

If Susan Beck suffers from a lack of space her husband also, it seems, could easily manage an acre or two besides his parochial obligations as both priest and organist. In the Becks' small drawing-room facing directly onto a quiet but centrally situated street in the town, solid bookshelves, laden with books and gramophone records, crowd the dark upright piano. Sheet music and plant catalogues happily coexist. Melody emanates from this household, and harmony exudes from the garden.

Susan Beck has crowded into her part of the garden a collection of roses and hardy geraniums living hugger-mugger in a seemingly random array of narrow borders and small island beds. This style of gardening comes directly from the heart, from an urge to go on adding plants where other less spirited gardeners might pause and say, 'enough'.

Poppies and delphiniums, Little Tulsa

Much the same occurs below in Father Beck's domain. Here, in summer, the network of rolled-cinder pathways is obscured by a galaxy of mostly hardy perennial plants flourishing in the long narrow enclosed garden. As members of the Hardy Plant Society the Becks naturally include a number of rarer species and cultivars, but these are not chosen for any exclusiveness or quirky botanical appearance: they must have a showy, almost a bright and cheery, countenance of their own. This is a happy party; down-in-the-dumps with sulky habits are not admitted.

There is a cottage-garden effect here, created partly by the inclusion, or rather remains, of vegetables and old fruit trees. Currant bushes and rhubarb hold their own against towering delphiniums, the smaller gunnera (*Gunnera chilensis*, syn. *G. tinctoria*) and crusading banners of *Rheum palmatum*. Cottage-garden favourites proliferate: hostas, peonies, daisies, a double-flowered hardy geranium and a kaleidoscope of familiars recognisable to generations of country gardeners.

Colour, so important in this garden, comes not only from the deep blue delphiniums and clear geranium blues but also from less frequently-encountered specimens like *Cynoglossum nervosum* and the dark purple *Malva mauritiana*, punctuated with the strong yellows of daisy-like *Inula magnifica*, and several forms of ligularia.

Paler, more discreet colour issues from plants which, oddly, stand well against their flamboyant neighbours. Poppies in smoky shades of purplish grey associate well with the similar hues found in *Salvia turkestanica*. The curious greyish-pink flowers of *Campanula lactiflora* 'Loddon Anna' seen with grey-leaved artemisias smoulder here and there.

If this wealth of plants begins to activate an acquisitive streak in visitors, it can be gratified with the knowledge that Father Beck is a great propagator who on most open days can offer unusual plants for sale, with the proceeds adding extra funds to the church coffer.

The house from the lower garden, Little Tulsa

Perhaps John Beck learnt about colour from his father, a stained-glass restorer whose work on the East Window of Gloucester Cathedral after the last war was highly valued. Or perhaps he discovered colour on his own and taught himself to apply it with such confidence. Whichever way it was, the results are uplifting and together, churchman and wife, Father and Mrs Beck have imposed upon these few square yards a brightness which is sure to last their tenancy and perhaps influence future incumbents.

MRS DAVID VEREY

BARNSLEY HOUSE

Barnsley, Gloucestershire

A part of Barnsley House garden's reputation stems from Rosemary Verey's unflagging enthusiasm for people, rivalled only by her insatiable quest for worthwhile old gardening books and first-rate plants. People *are* inseparable from gardens, despite what garden photographers (or their publishers) may think, and I cannot recall a single instance when I have been to Barnsley House and not met either a garden writer, painter or photographer, or someone like me who is professionally involved with horticultural publishing. Anyone who is anyone in gardening has passed through these gates.

This is one of Britain's best known private gardens, featured in countless magazines all over the world. For serious foreign garden visitors Barnsley House lies on the pilgrim's road which leads from the ramparts of Sissinghurst Castle to the front door of Hidcote Manor, and it is quite possible to stand on Barnsley's narrow *potager* paths and be 'excuse me'd' in half a dozen languages in one afternoon.

Who is Rosemary Verey? What is the allure of her garden?

David and Rosemary Verey went to live at Barnsley House in 1951. They had a young and growing family which meant that the valuable outdoor space was initially better utilised as cricket ground and grazing land for ponies. But as children grew up time became available for other pursuits. Charles, the elder son, imaginative for a teenager, gave his mother a subscription to the Royal Horticultural Society as a Christmas present in 1960, and her younger daughter gave her a large empty notebook labelled 'Your Gardening Book'. Seeds, so to speak, were sown.

Barnsley House was built in 1697. David Verey's parents lived there

The Temple, Barnsley House

before them, and when Rosemary took up the border fork for the first time there she recognised the value of the 'surrounding walls . . . trees more than one hundred years old, yew hedges and yards of box planted in the nineteenth century' as the welcoming bones awaiting renewed flesh. This of course was the 'silver spoon' birth of a gardener in early middle age destined to become, thirty years on, today's horticultural celebrity known to millions of people who have not, in many cases, ever set foot on these shores, let alone paid to tread the 'familiar' Barnsley paths.

Fortunately Rosemary Verey has kept a gardening diary down the years. It is so easy to forget when a particular tree was planted, where it came from or, indeed, how much it cost. These are not trivial matters but the stuff of garden history, and our information about medieval and later gardens has been much bolstered by similar forms of everyday account.

In the early diaries (extracts from which I was pleased to publish in *Hortus*) there are repeated references to plants seen at the Royal Horticultural Society's regular London shows, and anyone today can still learn a great deal more from a couple of uncrowded visits to Vincent Square than from any amount of time spent at the Chelsea Flower Show. Books, naturally, inspired Mrs Verey as well; she has in print paid her debt to Russell Page (*The Education of a Gardener*, 1962), to Vita Sackville-West, and to the now almost-forgotten Theo. Stephens whose journal, *My Garden*, ran monthly from the early 1930s, with some interruption during the war, to the end of 1951. Not surprisingly Rosemary Verey herself began writing – books in which she passes on barrowloads of practical information useful to gardeners in many temperate countries. She travels everywhere, it seems, and recently judged flower shows in America where she is a constant visitor and popular lecturer.

The garden as we know it today began with the planting of the Wilderness, an area on the south-west side of the house where previously David Verey's mother had long herbaceous borders backed by yew hedges next to rough grass with a few daffodils. For me this is one of Mrs Verey's triumphs, to be seen at its best around Easter with paths freshly mown between narcissi, primroses and celandines bejewelled with sky-blue speedwells. I first saw this part of the garden

Late summer, Barnsley House

in flower only last year; despite all my numerous visits I must have missed out on April previously. Shade in this part of the garden comes from *Prunus* 'Ukon', *P. sargentii*, and *P.* 'Tai Haku', the Great White cherry, all of which abandon their snowy petals on the yellow carpet in spring and, later, add to an array of autumn leaf colour immodestly broadcast by *Sorbus* 'Embley', *Parrotia persica*, ginkgo, *Cornus mas* (provider of yet more springtime yellow) and a crab apple (*Malus toringoides*) whose multitude of bead-like amber-yellow fruits linger long after the leaves have dropped.

Rosemary Verey has striven for contrast in her four cultivated acres, and this is noticeable particularly when the Wilderness is seen from over the knot garden, a small formal 'apron' threaded with wall germander (*Teucrium chamaedrys*) and box with central bosses of phillyrea. Before Mrs Verey moved to her 'dower' quarters on the other side of the house, she was able to look out on the sinuous knot from the drawing-room where her work was spread over a number of book-laden tables. Originally the knot was appropriately surrounded with a rosemary hedge, but this perished in severe cold one year and no replacement has been planted although clipped yellow-and-green-variegated hollies have been placed in the corners.

Another knot runs out from the door of a room which used to be Mrs Verey's kitchen, and the lattice work of criss-cross box remains planted with culinary herbs. In summer the pattern is lost under billowing sages, mists of fennel, dill and lovage and dozens of other essential flavourings for soups and salads, grand dinners and happy impromptu snacks. Crowded around the old kitchen door, by a wall bearing a great sail of *Rosa longicuspis* (the same species which fills the centre of the White Garden at Sissinghurst Castle), pots of geraniums (pelargoniums), fuchsias and curious black-faced aeoniums spend a cosseted summer vacation.

Pots also huddle around the garden door which leads from the drawing-room, now part of Charles Verey and his wife Denzil's domain. The wide stone path leading from this door to a gate in the far wall – roughly bisecting the garden – is thick with helianthemums in summer, reminding me of those bright floral pavements got up for Corpus Christi in Spain, except those are in strict patterns. Clipped upright yews are positioned down the path and these help to emphasise the distance from one end to the other.

The main flower beds at Barnsley are fit to be seen at any time of the year, but have not been planted to amuse the casual visitor who craves, or sometimes demands, his penn'orth of 'colour'. One bleak day I noticed a pool of yellow dogs'-tooth violets, 'Pagoda' I think, under the bare branches of two weeping cherries. They were not signposted, I don't think they were even labelled; they were half hidden, tucked away, and therefore all the more thrilling to find.

On another occasion I arrived late one afternoon from Wales in midwinter with a friend who had not seen the garden before, and Rosemary Verey whisked the pair of us round the garden in the dark,

The marrow tunnel, Barnsley House

picking out sumptuous clumps of hellebores, early jonquils and fronds of yellow jasmine with the beam of her torch. I was not surprised to see a few years later that she had written *The Garden in Winter* (1988), a book well designed to wrench 'fair weather' gardeners from the comfort of their December and January fireside chairs.

At the end of the first instalment of 'The making of an English Garden' (*Hortus* 8), Rosemary Verey lists over *fifty* specific plants or groups of plants flowering nowadays at Barnsley House between January and March. They range from a multitude of bulbs – scillas, snowdrops, crocuses, small irises, muscari and species tulips – to winter-flowering herbaceous perennials including bergenias, primulas, pansies, violas and pulmonarias, through to shrubs such as witch hazel, wintersweet (*Chimonanthus praecox*), garrya, and one or two roses which had not suffered autumn-wielded secateurs. The Cotswolds, remember, are not known for mild winters, so this list not only illustrates the benefit of walls and trees as shelter, it also demonstrates the results of careful planning and what might simply be called good gardening.

Sitting on a chair or bench among your plants is much advocated by Rosemary Verey; in her seventieth year she wrote: 'There is a limit to the amount of physical work I can do in the garden, and anyway time spent just sitting or walking round contemplating the next move is time well spent, in fact it is an essential part of gardening.' This is particularly true of someone whose brain, eyes and hands must combine to direct an indispensable team consisting of the young brothers Andy and Les Bailey, Rosemary Hughes and Sue le Fleming, with extra help at busier times depending on the season. If this appears to be a large work-force, you must examine the extent to which these acres are exploited and bear in mind, too, that there is also a small but thriving nursery. No one would describe Barnsley House as having a labour-saving garden.

Bulbs are used generously. There is no herbaceous border in the true sense of the words and, as we have seen, the bulbs bring colour to beds and borders from the first day of the year. Annuals and biennials, too, are used to extend seasonal plantings here and there. Some are raised in boxes, others may be planted *in situ* to flower the following year.

One of the principal flower borders at Barnsley House runs parallel with the Lime Walk, continuing as the Laburnum Walk to the far edge of the garden. The pebbles set in the path under the laburnums are from beaches in south Wales, laid by David Verey when the trees were first planted. Constructed of *Tilia platyphyllos* 'Rubra', the Lime Walk, dark and mysterious in leaf, takes on a different character in winter when the previous season's twigs glow red. These are left to catch the winter sun, then trimmed to shape in early March just before a new crop of leaves breaks bud. The Laburnum Walk, entwined with wisterias and one *Clematis orientalis* 'Bill Mackenzie', is underplanted each side with tall purply *Allium aflatunense* chosen to flower at the precise moment when the laburnums are letting down their yellow tresses.

The two rows of limes and laburnums form part of one of the three long vistas in the garden; at one end the eye stops at an upright piece of masonry carrying a memorial plaque to Rosemary's husband. Another vista, of grass this time, runs parallel to the tunnel and stops

The Laburnum Walk, Barnsley House

into a resplendent ballroom at a time when further alterations for Lord Eldon were undertaken by Sydney Tatchell.

The Eldon seat was in Dorset and the family used Stowell Park principally as a shooting lodge; the present Lord Vestey's grandparents came here in the 1920s. Celia Vestey arrived in 1981 and she recalls watching the Polish-born gardener, Mark Szymkowiak, supervising the planting of the summer bedding, as rigorously geometric as it must have been since the days before the First World War when her grandmother-in-law decided how things were done. It seems that Stowell was completely bypassed by the Arts and Crafts movement, and lasted into the penultimate decade of this century as a Victorian garden untouched by many of the styles and practices which influenced other Cotswold gardens. In slightly less than ten years, since Lady Vestey made this her home, she has introduced new thinking and new plantings, while preserving the unmistakable old character which seems still to emanate from the 'village' of structures, including a church, scattered behind the large house.

Oliver Leach came to Stowell Park as Head Gardener in the 1930s and died a short time ago at the age of 92. For part of that time Gordon Blinco, another invaluable gardener, worked here with Mark Szymkowiak (a soldier and German prisoner of war rehabilitated to this country) who has only recently retired.

Approaching today between diagonally-set stone Gate Houses, built in 1880 – one draped in roses 'Paul's Himalayan Musk' and 'The Garland' – you walk or drive to the house along an avenue of pleached limes planted as recently as 1983. These have already acquired sufficient stature to stand on their own, and with their individual stakes now removed they no longer have that infant look which new schemes like this all too often carry for so long. The first branches, more than six feet high above bare trunks, are knitting together well, and like a chain of human beings linking arms to demonstrate strength, each tree adds to the sturdiness of the whole row.

The broad terrace on the south side of the house overlooks the River Coln, and the Chedworth Woods face you across the valley; below, the paved terrace drops some twenty feet to a grassed area. An existing Victorian engraving shews that an Italianate garden was once proposed for this 'sunken' site; there is no evidence to suggest it was ever

On the terrace, Stowell Park

actually made, but the drops and levels remain intact should the present or future owners decide to install such a thing. At the end of 1990 plans to 'support' the retaining wall with yew buttresses were being put into action.

Rosemary Verey has helped with the planting on the terrace in recent years. A long border filled mainly with herbaceous plants runs hard against the balustrading for the entire length. Clumps of rugosa roses and cistuses grow on the terrace between the house and the long border, and purple sage, santolina and alchemilla, violas and variegated arabis have been planted or have seeded themselves about in the cracks. Diascias and felicias tumble out of stone troughs. Urns are planted with neat, clipped shapes.

A path leads to a seventeenth-century gabled dovecot, and the high bank which shelters it from the north is planted up with bulbs, wild flowers and shrubs beneath the trees to create a bowery effect which is simultaneously a sound ecological habitat for small birds, mammals and insects.

I like very much the way in which hard corners of the house or garden walls have been softened with mounds of sprawling roses or imaginatively-placed jasmines. These somehow sweeten your progress and enliven what might otherwise be 'dead' areas. Quite another effect transports visitors to the walled garden: the Dark Walk contains a path beneath clean-stemmed hollies underplanted with snowdrops, hellebores, cyclamen species and gauzy ferns.

There *is* a 'village' atmosphere at Stowell Park, and little pathways connect the cottages, greenhouses and outbuildings and the small twelfth-century church, all to the north of the house. Rising to this new level, you come across a pair of gravelled beds where unusual bulbs are grown. Almost immediately you are in the Cutting Garden, which is crammed with a vast array of mostly herbaceous flowers to be picked in great quantity for the house throughout the spring and summer and into autumn. Twenty different phloxes, ten kinds of peony, fifteen delphinium cultivars, campanulas, anthemis, monarda, scabious, verbascums, echinops, alstroemerias and more roses are all crammed together with *Lilium regale*, achilleas, sedums, acanthus and *Sidalcea* 'Elsie Heugh' (offered by only a handful of English nurseries). For cut foliage there are choisya, dark-stemmed *Hebe* 'Mrs Winder', rosemary and teucrium (*T. fruticans*, with silver, almost white stems that carry the palest of lavender flowers early in the year).

The lean-to glass structures running along the high, brick-lined east-facing walls are stately in their length, bountiful with their produce. Here white-fleshed peaches, not grown widely in this country now, reach a degree of size, ripeness and profusion which could easily send giddy the most ambitious of London greengrocers. Old vines bearing trusses of sweet grapes create important dappled shade. The Stowell Park breakfast and dining tables must be the envy of the county. Add to these delicate fruits great quantities of sticky figs, and it was not surprising to learn that greenhouse duties are sought eagerly by casual and full-time garden staff alike.

In other greenhouses there are huge displays of pot plants. 'Apple-blossom' geraniums stand out among another variety called 'Arctic

A first glimpse of the garden, Stowell Park

Star' whose little chalky flowers are so appropriately named. Scented carnations rise on staked stems above their glaucous foliage.

In the vegetable beds proper there is what might almost be described as an antique asparagus bed. It is in three distinct sections – sixty, forty and twenty years old, respectively – and supplies trugsful of delicate-tasting spears in early summer, while the subsequent haze of mid-green foliage acts as a refined backdrop to the flowers in adjacent rectangles.

In neat rows among the vegetables are lines and lines of caned chrysanthemums stood out in parade-ground order, in colours ranging from white through pink and yellow, to deep red and curious browns. Their names seem to belong to a separate world with a hint of the show-bench: 'Long Island', 'Pink Marble', 'Bronze Medallion' and 'Yellow Galaxy'; somehow, they could not be roses. Much neglected or even maligned by some gardeners, these late-summer flowering plants, when well grown, *à la* Stowell, remind us what great pleasure their prodigality gives, and what glowing richness their picked blooms can bring to fire-lit rooms at a moment in the year when celery appears for tea, and curtains are drawn before six.

The Kitchen Garden is full of wonders and unlikely incident. A new rose tunnel crosses the whole area, like a floral highway, left to right. Two people can walk abreast upon a hard path edged with gravel and bordered by a low box hedge. They will pass between and under some of the best roses man has bred: 'Parkdirektor Riggers', 'Madame Alfred Carrière', 'Sanders' White', 'Madame Grégoire Staechelin', 'Félicité et Perpétue', 'François Juranville', Climbing 'Iceberg', and 'Albéric Barbier' at the centre. Among these pedigree roses are a few equally seductive but less well-known varieties including 'Princess Louise' (similar to 'Félicité et Perpétue' and bred by the same nurseryman in France a year later, in 1828); 'Allen Chandler', a climbing Hybrid Tea from America; 'Weetwood', a self-sown seedling of Old Rose character found recently in a Devonshire garden; and 'Alexandre Girault', a red Rambler with a green eye and yellow stamens dating from the Edwardian period.

A new, deep, west-facing herbaceous border has been installed at the top of the Kitchen Garden beneath another long run of high, warm, red brick wall, and nearby a circle of yellow-flowered roses has been planted over the past year or two; this is a unique feature and one worthy of emulation, with alterations made to suit anyone's fancy. At Stowell this imaginative circle – some twenty feet across – cut out of grass, rising in the centre but not uniformly like a pudding, is composed primarily of the paler yellows. 'Windrush', *R. pimpinellifolia*, 'Graham Thomas', 'Goldfinch', 'Leverkusen', 'Yellow Button', 'Nevada', *R. hugonis*, 'Agnes', and 'Mary Webb' are laced up together, with *Anthemis tinctoria* 'Wargrave Variety' and touches of blue *Campanula latiloba*. I stood back for some minutes to appreciate the effect of this sunny circle, and I would like to think of it as the manifestation of one person's nightlong pursuit of a dozen rose catalogues.

Yet more roses adorn a large fruit cage containing all the soft fruits which must be netted against the birds and, perhaps, the odd hungry garden visitor. Rising out of surrounding hyssop, rosemary and nepeta are 'Old Blush China' and 'Wife of Bath', proving that nothing at Stowell is left unadorned.

This garden is not open frequently; it is very much a private world, enjoyed and enriched by its owners and its staff. Ghosts of Victorian gardeners in leather aprons might be watching your every move, the spectres of old men deft at hand pollination in the peach house might interrupt your stroll, or you could just as easily be confronted by the vision of a strict but gracious lady directing the hands of her gardeners as they assemble the season's bedding-out in a range of colours not likely to be found in the real Stowell Park of today. Whatever the illusion, whatever your reaction, be sure to bring a notebook to record what you see. Unlike me, you may not be fortunate enough to be told everything by Mr Hewertson who, doubtless, will be in some corner ensuring that yet a few more square yards of this remarkable garden will spring to bloom in another season.

COTSWOLD FARM

Near Cirencester, Gloucestershire

Well-named, Cotswold Farm lies discreetly to one side of the busy Swindon-to-Gloucester road not far from Cirencester. It remains to this day an active farm snug in its own valley. Major Birchall, a keen plantsman himself, is not the only gardening member of his family: his sister Mary is chatelaine of Rodmarton Manor. Ruth Birchall is today's gardener at Cotswold Farm where earlier her parents-in-law, Sir John and Lady Birchall, first put the place in order when they moved from Bowden Hall near Gloucester in 1926.

I feel a positive sense of arriving at a proper working estate immediately I turn off the main road. The pair of cottages on the left has been embellished with a row of clipped limes which at once lift them from the ordinary. The large walled kitchen garden forms an island – an oasis almost – in the approach drive which brings visitors round the back of the rambling house to the main courtyard entrance on the north-east side. This paved yard with low clipped box hedges and topiary is spangled in September and October with pure white Japanese anemones which have seeded themselves profusely into every possible crevice.

If you do not enter the garden by passing through the seventeenth-century house, you will most likely emerge on the first of several terraces through a little gate opening by one of two wings added to the building by Sidney Barnsley in 1926. There, falling in a series of levels, is the range of terraces whose grand proportions are unmistakably Edwardian in inspiration. Actually, they were begun in 1938, but belong in every other way to that peak in English garden-making history.

In the terrace garden in Autumn, Cotswold Farm

A generously wide terrace of the same grey Cotswold stone follows the south-east-facing walls of the house to a garden room where semi-circular steps lead down from a centrally-placed door. Here among the paving cracks are hundreds of self-sown daisy-like erigerons, dwarf campanulas, helianthemums and low, spreading thymes sprawling before two mounds of rosemary. Beyond, just a few paces away, the White Border benefits from a high wall at its back offering the best possible protection for a delightful stretch of pale planting. This border displays white-flowering bulbs with creamy hellebores and white pulmonarias below snowy cherry blossom in spring, succeeded in the summer months by white cistuses, peonies and tall milky campanulas, with silvery highlights shining from white-edged hosta leaves, *Convolvulus cneorum*, 'Miss Willmott's Ghost' and *Stachys lanata*. The rose 'Seagull' acts as a white curtain in midsummer, and its slightly glaucous foliage looks good even when the flowers have finished.

On the front of this terrace is a low yew hedge which seems to sit atop the wall, serving as a backdrop to the terrace below. By descending central steps flanked by two six-tiered pieces of columnar box topiary, you enter the widest and most formal terrace, designed

advisers (call them what you will) to make recommendations by post for schemes, having first been supplied by the principal agent with details of soil type, climate, topography, et cetera.

In addition to the two flower borders at Combend, Miss Jekyll also made a plan to improve the pondside planting, using many of her favourite shrubs including laurustinus (*Viburnum tinus*), skimmias, Portugal laurel and berberis species, underplanted with fritillaries and colchicums. (The plan for this scheme is now in the Reef Point Gardens Collection, University of California, Berkeley.) The two borders still exist, and the planting around what is now one of five ponds looks, not perhaps surprisingly, mature.

Today's plan lists twenty-one distinct garden areas: a considerably fussier layout than that conceived by Mr Barnsley, whose original plan also still exists. Many of the 'gardens within gardens' are quite small and devoted to single ideas, such as a grass garden, and beds used for growing cut flowers and annuals for drying.

On a raised terrace is the White Garden, enclosed on three sides by house and outbuildings. Facing south, it is ideally positioned to retain warmth and gain protection from unfriendly north and east winds. 'Iceberg' floribunda roses and the Hybrid Tea 'Pascali' occupy the four square beds, with frothy ground-hugging *Artemisia schmidtiana* beneath them. Shrubs are trained on the walls and where, as with *Cytisus battandieri*, their flowers are not white, the silvery-grey leaves carry the theme.

The Cedar Lawn is named for its dominant *Cedrus deodara*, but other fine trees coexist happily. A weeping ash (*Fraxinus excelsior* 'Pendula'), a purple beech and an old black mulberry all add their mark to the lawn and throw some afternoon shade onto the Spring Garden, where circular paving slabs act as stepping stones through the close planting. As its name suggests, this border is best in the early months when snowdrops, hellebores, scillas, and pulmonarias sparkle in weak sunshine.

The Spring Border leads into the Silver Border, where foliage is the main concern. *Artemisia* 'Powis Castle' and *Eucalyptus gunnii* (pollarded yearly to encourage the smaller, lighter, almost blue juvenile leaves) are well surrounded with pungent *Helichrysum angustifolium*, the curry plant, exuding its powerful scent on warm days to be carried throughout the garden on the slightest breeze.

An area which once accommodated the family swimming pool has been replanted with shrubs and small trees that colour well in autumn. In October, the russet leaves of *Rhus typhina* 'Laciniata' and the glowing tones of snowy mespilus (*Amelanchier lamarckii*) set off beautifully the bright yellow fruits of 'Golden Hornet' crab apples and the pinkish-white berries of *Sorbus hupehensis*.

Sidney Barnsley's delightful dovecot arch forms the break in Miss Jekyll's borders, which flank it left and right. This is the Miss Jekyll of the graded colour schemes. At the top (north) end her well-known spectrum begins with the greys, lilacs, purples and pale yellows melting into shades of pink and white, then leading into more robust hues of yellow and fiery oranges and reds. The colours repeat themselves in reverse order through the 'twin' border so that the dovecot arch, made of stone with a sandy pigment, is embraced in the middle by the strongest shades. The borders are planted to this day with many of the plants which were originally specified. Replacements for the few which have died out have proved difficult to track down, but the half-and-half, perennial/annual, mix is composed of heleniums, delphiniums, thalictrums, *Aster acris, Chrysanthemum uliginosum*, salvias, echinops and bergamot; antirrhinums, French and African marigolds, dahlias and hollyhocks. The rose 'Zéphirine Drouhin' on

Betula jacquemontii avenue, Combend Manor

the arch itself is perhaps out of place with its almost shocking-pink blooms; it was certainly well-known and much planted by the early decades of this century, but was it Miss Jekyll's choice?

Facing the Jekyll borders are two shrub borders of similar size, but wholly different in spirit. Not yet ten years old, these billow already with *Choisya ternata*, variegated fuchsias, a purple-leaved smoke bush (from an earlier scheme), and *Buddleia davidii* 'Dartmoor' whose purplish-red flowers appear in large flat panicles. A collection of named viola cultivars and some herbaceous perennials are employed to cover any patches of bare earth. Behind the shrubs are the Cutting Beds and next to this roses are grown in a small yew-enclosed garden crossed by paths of grass. 'Buff Beauty', 'Celestial' and the stripey-petalled 'Ferdinand Pichard' are fronted with a hedge of 'Little White Pet' which flowers away reliably all summer long and well into the autumn months.

Below is the Croquet Lawn surrounded with borders planted up in shades of red. Clumps of tall miscanthus and several *Aralia elata* have been included to add height. This Japanese angelica tree, introduced to Britain in about 1830, has large panicles of white flowers in early autumn and its showy leaves flutter like banners above the bloody annual and herbaceous subjects.

The Main Pond is the first in a chain of five which descend to the lowest levels. Moorhens have made for themselves a home beneath the seemingly impenetrable wide-spreading branches of *Juniperus pfitzeriana*. In springtime the pond's banks are crowded with kingcups, skunk cabbages and primulas. In the autumn, pheasants bred on the estate cackle among the first leaves to fall from the the variegated sycamore and tall *Acer pseudoplatanus* 'Leopoldii'.

Good trees have established themselves around all the ponds, and further beyond them is the Arboretum, with younger specimens coming on well. Unusual beeches grow here, and a grove of dawn redwoods (*Metasequoia glyptostroboides*) provides light gauzy green colour in the spring and burnished tints in the autumn.

Back at the top, by the Old Vegetable Garden, a double row of twelve young *Betula jacquemontii*, the Himalayan birch, with the whitest possible stems of papery peeling bark, leads the eye right out of the garden and over the fields to a broadleaved wood providing as perfect a view and contrast as could be desired.

MISARDEN PARK

Miserden, Gloucestershire

M isarden Park, grey but welcoming, stands with the hamlet of
Miserden scattered around its northern brim. The wide terrace
on the south-east front faces a typical Cotswold valley, deeply riven,
wooded for centuries. The house has been altered several times since
it was built in 1620 for Sir William Sandys. An engraving by the
Dutchman Johannes Kip (1653–1722) shows a five-gabled house with
three projecting bays surrounded by formal terracing with a parterre
and rows of evenly-spaced trees. The present owner's grandfather
came here in 1914 and made alterations which were followed by yet
more work – by Sir Edwin Lutyens this time – after a fire caused
damage to the east wing in 1919. Lutyens linked his new wing to the
main house with an arched loggia which remains to this day as a cool
retreat in summer.

The wide stone terrace has replaced what Kip shews as a level
grassed or gravelled plat with four rectangular beds surrounded by
balustrading. More of a natural, landscaped, look has returned to the
areas close to the house today, although the site occupied by the
present Kitchen and Rose Gardens can be seen clearly on the old
engraving. Kip made his images as if from somewhere above the
tree-tops, and these 'bird's-eye' views are a valuable record of how a
number of estates in the county looked when Sir Robert Atkyns
commissioned the engravings for his *Ancient and Present State of Glos-
tershire* (1712).

The way to see Misarden today is to enter beside the great
horse-chestnut and make your way slowly between a pair of herbaceous borders which must be among the largest in Britain. They slope

gently towards the house and are crossed about half way by a path which reveals a sudden glimpse of other parts to be explored. Each of these borders is approximately three hundred feet long and thirty feet wide, and crammed with an enormous variety of plants grouped in bold clumps to help manage the scale.

Running parallel with the whole length of the borders is the Yew Walk, whose top is cut in bold arcs like domed castellations. Because of its great length it appears narrower than it really is, disappearing at one end to what seems like a pinprick of an urn on a plinth. At the end nearest the house the walk terminates in a pair of stone piers topped with ball finials and holding an ironwork gate of handsome and intricate design.

Silver and Grey Borders flank a short flight of steps which transports strollers to the main terrace level. The greys and silvers come from santolina, senecio and pinks, and standing one atop each pillar are three-foot lead statues of a boy and a girl – he calling the tune on two pipes while she twirls with scarf above her head. Below them there are more grey foliage plants enlivened with the yellowy greens of euphorbia and tall fennels. A few irises sound a blue note briefly, and pink roses join the two levels with their flowery limbs. We are now on the broad terrace looking south-east towards the woods.

The house has been softened with wisterias, honeysuckles and clematis. Five massive blocks of clipped yew stand near the edge of the terrace where there is a fall in the lie of the land. In summer, flowering for several months, the great spectacle is the long row of nepeta whose bluey haze appears like a sea on which the whole house sails. Buddleias and pale pink roses punctuate the catmint at regular intervals, blending the entire planting scheme with the dominant building.

As the ground falls away even further there are steps cut in the grass, the risers planted with blue and white alyssum – a mowing nightmare perhaps, but worth every effort. The same idea is repeated in another part of the garden and it is possible it may date from the time when Lutyens worked here.

At the far end of the terrace there is a great spray of white crambe disappearing into a border full of white rosebay willow-herb (*Epilobium angustifolium* 'Album'). To the northwards under a mature magnolia is

The house above the terrace, Misarden Park

the Butler's Walk, planted with pleached hornbeams, and low-growing herbaceous plants and bulbs which can get along without a constant need for sunlight.

The Rose Garden occupies ground between the Yew Walk and a high boundary wall. It is the size of a couple of tennis courts and holds a collection of both Victorian and modern roses. Newly installed *treillage* divides the roses from the Kitchen Garden which is worked in a traditional way with crops planted in rows, rotating appropriately.

From the Kitchen Garden it is possible to take the crossing path which cuts through the Yew Walk and divides the herbaceous borders. If you continue across you pass under a rose pergola, through a gate leading to wilder parts of the garden. Through the wrought-iron gate there is a view back to the Kitchen Garden which gives no indication of the enormous size of the beds running left and right. Two lead cisterns filled with agapanthus stand like dwarf sentries either side of the gate.

Out in the less formal areas the grass is allowed to grow longer and

Figure in the garden, Misarden Park

wild flowers are beginning to establish themselves. There are some good specimen trees: *Fagus sylvaticum* 'Purpurea', the copper beech, *Catalpa bignonioides*, walnut (*Juglans regia*), and *Davidia involucrata*, the pocket-handkerchief tree whose seeds require a double period of stratification before they will germinate.

On yet more falling ground there is the Arboretum, which in Major Wills' grandmother's day was a giant rockery. Now almost no labour is required to keep the trees in order and tidy up occasionally around the *Cornus controversa* 'Variegata', the cercidiphyllum from Japan with what has been described as 'smokey pink autumnal colouring', liquidambar (good autumn colour again), black mulberry and a weeping elm sprinkled through the pines and native broadleaf trees.

Misarden is another of those wonderful gardens which you may hope to leave carrying specimens of the plants you have seen and much admired. The nursery has a good range of hardy herbaceous plants, and glass-houses filled with regal pelargoniums, potted streptocarpus and an assortment of other plants which visitors without a garden can take away and enjoy.

INTERLUDE

III

Pinbury Park – Duntisbourne Rouse,
Gloucestershire
Brewers Cottage – Eastcombe, Gloucestershire
Painswick Rococo Garden – Painswick,
Gloucestershire

This Interlude takes us to three gardens which in terms of distance, if not style, are reasonably close to each other. The first and last lie each in its own private landscape, while the second is an example of one couple's approach to gardening around their own hillside cottage in a present-day village setting.

PINBURY PARK once belonged to a religious order based in Caen in northern France, and reports of seeing the ghost of a nun in the avenue of yews, or Nun's Walk, are still mentioned. Its former occupants have included Sir Robert Atkyns and the Poet Laureate, John Masefield. Ernest Barnsley and his wife lived there for a time and some of their friends and colleagues occupied cottages adapted from the outbuildings. Norman Jewson has written about that period: 'The house was in a bad state of repair, while the terraced gardens were jungles of every kind of weed and their walls dilapidated. . . . Six years after [the Barnsleys] had moved in, the new yew hedges had taken shape, lawns and flower borders were in perfect order and the house and buildings were in good repair and had the aspect once again of a fine old country house in a setting of great beauty.' That setting is unchanged, and Pinbury Park still seems remotely-situated, standing

Sheets of *Anemone blanda*, Pinbury Park

Topiary, Pinbury Park

in its own deeply-cleft section of the Frome valley between Cirencester and Bisley.

Mr and Mrs John Mullings live here now, and their garden presents
springtime visitors with one of the Cotswolds' most remarkable sights.
On ground rising from behind and to one side of the house there are
blankets of blue and white *Anemone blanda* through which the mower
must cut swathes so that wandering feet can be persuaded not to
trample too many flowers. Naturalisation on this scale cannot fail to
look impressive, but closer inspection reveals that there is more to the
picture than anemones. Primroses and celandines have wandered in
and their tones of yellow seem to strengthen the blueness of the blues
and give them more brilliant life.

There is good topiary, too, at Pinbury. It is cut with precision in late
summer ensuring crisp outlines throughout the winter and into
spring. The large sunken garden, planted with roses around the walls,
traps early sunshine. On a spring morning, with only rooks and crows
to invade the silence, it is possible here to imagine for a moment the

way much of the Cotswolds must have seemed before outbursts of ugly modern housing developments raped the countryside, and before ear-ripping motor engines destroyed the tranquillity of the lanes and the skies above. Lucky Pinbury; happy its springtime visitors.

We were attracted to BREWERS COTTAGE by the owners' description of their garden in the National Gardens Scheme's 'Yellow Book': 'Easily managed hillside garden with laburnum-covered pergola, shady & sunny borders and a small hidden courtyard. All year colour.' We were further intrigued to discover after a telephone call that the laburnum-covered pergola was not an imitation of various famous tunnels and arches constructed of at least twenty pairs of trees. There was, we were told, a *single* laburnum.

We were not disappointed by Brewers Cottage. I am sure it reflects the sort of garden Mr and Mrs Carter set out to make – unsullied by the dreadful stuff pumped out on some television gardening programmes. A hundred years ago this would have been a cottage garden in the true sense: straight rows of ubiquitous cabbages, potatoes, onions, peas and beans, with a few lupins, sweet peas and hollyhocks scattered where there was room. Some cottage gardens, made by people who have encountered the idea solely in books, are a poor realisation of what a true country cottage garden should be. Some of

The fountain in the hidden courtyard, Brewers Cottage

the books which advocate this style today will have you consulting the most adventurous seed and plant lists ever issued. The Carters have *not* missed the point, nor have they forgotten how years ago cottagers would very likely have kept a pig: at Brewers Cottage there are three fine porkers – each, I am pleased to say, rendered in non-sentient stone.

The Laburnum Pergola is pure joy. The one tree has been trained to climb between two columns and spread its branches over a few lateral supports. The results are ten or so square yards of hanging laburnum trusses in May providing much pleasure and satisfaction.

We had to ask about the 'small hidden courtyard', and I am glad we did. Its boundaries are various cottage and garden walls, and the only way into it is through the house. Hostas and kingcups luxuriate on the edge of a small pool, water splashes from the brimming bowl of a fountain, and the air is filled with the sweet perfume of honeysuckles scrambling up the walls. This is a secret place indeed, but one that lends its treasures to the whole house on warm days when casements are ajar.

The PAINSWICK ROCOCO GARDEN stands above the small town locally famous for its churchyard yews. Painswick House, Palladian in style, used once to be known as Buenos Aires. Its name has changed, but modern-day visitors can now see parts of the original garden, as they are restored, taking shape again among the winding paths, the well-sited viewing places and the detailed flourishes which adorn the buildings.

Writing in the summer 1988 issue of *Hortus* Paul Miles said that the garden 'is a rare survivor of a dizzy and exuberant style which is found in architectural decoration and has all but vanished out of doors.' He goes on to quote Bishop Pococke who went there in 1757:

We come to Painswick, a market town prettily situated on the side of the hill, and esteem'd an exceeding good air; just above it Mr. Hyett built an house of hewn stone, in a fine situation, and made a very pretty Garden; before it is a court with statues and sphynxes, and beyond that a lawn for the grand entrance; the Garden is on an hanging ground from the house in the vale, and on a rising ground on the other side and at the end; all are cut into walks through wood

Within the Red House, Painswick Rococo Garden

and adorn'd with water and buildings, and in one part is the kitchen garden.

The earliest depiction of this garden is by Thomas Robins (1716–1770) who may also have been responsible for the garden's original layout. Much of what Bishop Pococke saw over two hundred years ago can be seen today, thanks to the restoration undertaken by Lord and Lady Dickinson, who have approached their mission with gusto.

David Verey describes one of the garden buildings, the Red House, as having 'gay ogee curves', while another open-fronted gazebo consists of three arches and a castellated parapet.

There are ponds and a shrubbery and a fine collection of native and exotic trees. Snowdrops grow in abundance and each year the garden opens for these at the beginning of February. Old photographs exist shewing visitors who were once allowed to pick a dozen flowers, although this would not be encouraged today. (James Atkins, the

Alcove in Painswick Rococo Garden

snowdrop grower mentioned in my Introduction, lived at Rose Cottage, Painswick.)

To visit Painswick Rococo Garden is to receive a lesson in English garden history: walk its paths, appreciate its scale, enjoy echos of its former exuberance. Above all, give thanks for its continued existence.

133

MR AND MRS PETER WIMPERIS

WATER LANE FARM

Selsley, Gloucestershire

P eter and Gillian Wimperis have made their herb and goat farm on the slopes of a Stroud valley facing Rodborough Fort, which dates originally from the 1760s but was rebuilt a hundred years later.

Water Lane Farm, however, predates all this by several centuries. It has enjoyed uncluttered views (if a building can be said to enjoy views) since around 1550, although the last few decades have brought sad changes to this and other Cotswold valleys.

The farm is approached down a steep lane and across a cattle-grid, ending in a sharp left turn. Immediately you step from your car, assuming you have arrived thus, your nostrils will be assailed by fragrances and scents more usually associated with the dry hills of Provence than Gloucestershire. For here is a working herb farm and nursery, selling plants, essential oils, dried leaves and flowers. But unlike many nurseries you can see the plants growing around you in both a formal and a relaxed fashion.

The little garden facing west near the shop is on a hot dry site particularly suited to growing many aromatic plants, but the main herb garden is beyond it, facing east on a level platform cut into the bank. This spot, known as Dad's Garden, has been made to a plan drawn by Gillian Wimperis's father, published in *House & Garden* in 1935, to accompany an article about herb gardening by his wife Margaret Molyneux. The plan had been safely preserved in the family but never before made into a garden. It fondly commemorates dad, while another family thread is woven in by eighty-four year old Mrs Molyneux's recent move from Somerset to the garden cottage.

A white seat with lad's-love growing through it is a lovely sight in

Stock beds, Water Lane Farm

itself. Here in Dad's Garden, though, it is just one imaginative component of a summer-tangled formal garden some thirty feet square. I asked Mrs Wimperis if it was fanciful to suppose that the central, almost cloven-hoof-shaped, pair of beds signified her interest in goats. Alas, I was on quite the wrong track! No matter; the design is sound enough and, as with good herb gardens anywhere, use has been made of other flowering plants, including pinks and white mallows which always look well among predominantly grey foliage.

Most of the plants grown for cutting and seed lie in rows beyond the nursery. No design called for here, but the sheer joy of seeing tightly packed long lines of full-blown herbs on a warm summer afternoon was memorable indeed. It is worth chanting the names, which in themselves evoke their own pungency and, sometimes, faraway origins. There are two blocks of rows, and walking down the middle of the first block you encounter lavender, variegated rue, rosemary, curry plants (*Helichrysum angustifolium*), purple sage, narrow-leaved sage, wall germander, cotton-lavender, green and golden marjoram, golden sage, dwarf curry plants, thyme, more lavender, and borage. Returning up the other block: yarrow, chives, pinks, thyme, *Marjoram compactum*, *Salvia blancoana*, winter savory, common thyme again, lemon thyme, sorrel, tarragon, and wild marjoram. Anyone even fleetingly acquainted with herbs will be able to conjure up the gently-hued colours and contrasts, let alone the fragrances emanating from this field.

But it is not all herbs at Water Lane Farm. There is a natural-looking but wholly man-made pond, and a Buddleia Grove too, a piece of land on the edge of the property where a collection of these late-summer flowering shrubs attracts every butterfly for miles around in July and August. One ingenious planting idea I have not previously encountered is the Lavender Fan; the design is made up of alternate radiating ribs of light 'Munstead' and dark 'Hidcote' lavender which happily flower at the same time to form a gauzy open fan some twenty feet wide. There are roses, too: old roses such as 'Tuscany Superb'; the strongly-perfumed repeat-flowering rugosa 'Roseraie de l'Haÿ'; the ancient Gallica 'Rosa Mundi'; 'Cécile Brunner', the 'Sweetheart Rose', exquisite in bud and flower; striped 'Ferdinand Pichard'; and another rugosa, 'Fimbriata', whose petals seem to have been trimmed with pinking shears. Around their feet are mounds of wayward catmint enlivened here and there with our old friend *Alchemilla mollis*. All these occupy a pair of newly-dug long borders running down the hillside near the goat-houses.

Dad's Garden, Water Lane Farm

thank her by leaving a few of the rooted specimens behind when we saw her on a later occasion.

The mixture of flowers at April Cottage prevents anyone from categorising Mary Dyer's interests. You will never leave her garden saying 'ah, she's an alpine fancier', 'golly, a foliage-freak', or 'wow! what weird weeds'. Early spring bulbs are carefully chosen to extend the season for as long as possible, starting as soon as the carpet of snowdrops by the garage has finished. Winter-flowering jasmine and *Viburnum tinus* and *V. bodnantense* give pleasure in the cold months, followed soon by primroses, bluebells and other wild things like celandines which all have their place among the more obvious, 'choicer' garden plants. Summer brings *Lilium regale* 'Album' and white *Lilium candidum* to spike the frothy undergrowth around the pond where, at Easter time usually, the low retaining wall foams with London Pride. Spilling over the paths in summer are verbenas, rudbeckias, spires of thalictrum, valerian (a prolific but none the less welcome commoner in the Cotswolds), tansy, lavender, more hostas, dark-stemmed ligularias, asphodelines, dwarf delphiniums, tobacco plants and rarities like *Lysimachia ephemerum* with tall spikes of densely-packed greyish-white flowers above a good clump of glaucous foliage.

One of Mrs Dyer's tricks last summer was to scatter cosmos seeds through the beds in late June or early July, much later than the instructions on the seed packet suggest. But Mary had the seeds and wasn't going to waste them; in September she was rewarded with a mist of these delicate flowers sailing above their ferny foliage and over the heads of *Aster × frikartii* 'Mönch', *Aster lateriflorus horizontalis*, and the unusual Texan, *Gaura lindheimeri* (all from Beth Chatto's Essex nursery). This little triumph lasted through October and well into November.

You will not be surprised to learn that Mary, having utilised all her available ground space, has now embarked upon 'vertical gardening'. In addition to a Climbing 'Iceberg' rose on the sunny wall of the cottage, a *Wisteria sinensis* has now been planted, and I have no doubt that under the discipline of Mary's green fingers this will wrap itself abundantly around the building in no time at all. Just as the rose was finishing last year (Climbing 'Iceberg' does not repeat itself like its shrub namesake), palest yellow hollyhocks came into their own, grown

Beansticks, April Cottage

from seed ultimately derived from some collected by Roy Lancaster along the Georgian Military Highway some ten years ago. These prolific hollyhocks, thoroughly appropriate in a cottage garden, grew to nine feet last summer, well above the sill of the bedroom windows.

So much goes on in this garden that my notes about it could have made a book on their own; so many plants jostle each other, but their individual performances are never lost. It would be hell to go plant-shopping with Mary (without a fat wallet and a trailer fixed to the back of the car) and I can only say, affectionately, that she gardens the way she talks: non-stop!

MRS ANTHONY BIDDULPH

RODMARTON MANOR

Rodmarton, Gloucestershire

I love Rodmarton Manor. Its scale should daunt and frighten, but it does not. Its long borders, enclosed beds, wild garden, groves and orchard ought to scare one off with the thought of endless weeding, staking, pruning, mowing and scything, but instead whenever I go there I long to rummage in the toolshed, find the necessary implement, and make my own small contribution to the continued well-being of these few wonderful acres. And if I were lucky enough to work alongside the garden's owner I should learn a great deal: about plants and planting, about traditional English village goings-on, about the very nature of life at the Big House, and the history of a building and its contents made to the highest standards by artist-craftsmen whose skills are almost unknown today, or virtually unaffordable. For here the full-blown Arts and Crafts ideal is met head-on.

Manor house, fittings, furnishings and outbuildings, were here conceived in unison with the garden, which grew from identical thoughts and principles. On a casual glance it would be forgivable to assume that this colossal house had stood on its site for several centuries. But it is less than a hundred years old, and enjoys today the hard work and concern of the woman whose father-in-law caused it to be built. Mary Biddulph lives and gardens here, and she has added her own distinctive taste, passions and interests to those of her predecessors.

Lord Biddulph, a London banker, gave to his son Claud in 1894 the then crumbling Rodmarton estate. In 1909 Ernest Barnsley of Sapperton was commissioned to erect a new house complete with private chapel and garden loggias which took twenty years to build.

147

Summer-house, Rodmarton Manor

The Arts and Crafts movement was well under way by the turn of the century; Sir Edwin Lutyens and Gertrude Jekyll were making their impact, William Morris was a household name, and Charles Paget Wade (at Snowshill), Richard Norman Shaw, and Oliver Hill were all practising architects who had turned their backs on Victorian artistic piety.

The new Rodmarton Manor grew out of its own ground: estate workers dug and carried the local stone, masons cut and positioned it; craftsmen-carpenters took their timbers from the great trees there-abouts while the blacksmiths burnt the offcuts to generate heat to forge the latches and ironwork.

Claud Biddulph's wife, Margaret, had been taught horticulture at college where she met her future head gardener William Scrubey whose name is commemorated on a plaque in the garden. It was this first Mrs Biddulph who made the garden; some things have of course changed since her day. Inevitably plants have died or fallen foul of storms and nature's other vagaries, but the garden was fortunate when the Biddulphs' son Anthony took for his bride Mary Birchall, whose brother and sister-in-law at Cotswold Farm have also proved them-selves to be such good garden makers.

Colour appears at the very beginning of the year when winter aconites produce their vast annual carpet of thick yellow flowers under the beech trees by the great disc of greensward known as The Circle. Mrs Biddulph's beloved snowdrops, tucked into shady beds in the garden proper, will also be flowering at the same time. Her collection of these bulbs includes numerous species and cultivars, bringing much interest to the beds and borders long before most gardeners have even cottoned-on to spring's approach.

There are almost twenty separate garden areas at Rodmarton Manor, including the Holly Drive and the Beech Drive which, interchangeably, serve as entrance or exit.

At the furthest point from the house the Hornbeam Avenue forms a mighty nave. In spring, when new leaves are emerging, its loftiness appears to be increased by the thin penetrating sunlight; as the foliage bulks up, the internal space darkens and seems to contract. The adjoining Wild Garden hosts many of Mary Biddulph's treasured hollies growing among wild flowers and deep blue periwinkle.

Agapanthus and doorway, Rodmarton Manor

The pair of herbaceous borders, long and wide, has an altogether different mood. Their central stone path is edged in grass, and narrow grass paths running the whole length behind give easy access to the tall yew hedges at clipping time. These borders are interrupted along their course by a small sunken pool surrounded by evergreen screens concealing four stone seats. At the far end the little stone Summerhouse, exquisite in every detail, is neatly framed by the thick screen of trees planted in the garden's early days and now grown to woodland proportions.

The large Kitchen Garden lies behind the herbaceous borders. Fruits and vegetables are grown in quantity, not only for the house and Mrs Biddulph's family, but also to be sent to Cirencester market to raise extra funds.

150

From the beginning this garden has accommodated growing children; tennis court and swimming pool have their place, but even these have not escaped the gardener's attention: one pavilion is now almost engulfed by *Rosa brunonii*. When I first visited this garden a few years ago, with Marco Polo Stufano and the late John Nally from Wave Hill garden in New York, John took cuttings – with Mrs Biddulph's permission – and one of the resulting plants now thrives in my garden in Wales while others, I trust, flourish in America.

The Cherry Orchard in spring is a remarkable sight. A rich variety of other shrubs and small trees, including *Parrotia persica*, grow among the *Prunus* species, and through early patches of snowdrops roses climb and sprawl without hindrance.

The Leisure Garden occupies a large rectangular area next to the west end of the house where the chapel is situated. Paths of stone and concrete intersect beds of roses and other shrubs with gold or grey and silver foliage. With no grass paths to mow, low maintenance guarantees the appropriateness of this little garden's name. It is overlooked by a sleeping-balcony, so placed as to catch every whiff of fragrance from the roses below on warm summer nights. Pleached limes, now with thick trunks, partly separate the Leisure Garden from the Troughery, the Winter Garden and the Topiary Garden. Mrs Biddulph's love of alpines has encouraged her to utilise many old farm troughs, now given new life as containers for a superb collection of low-growing plants. The Topiary Garden leads to the White Garden – a narrow border overlooking rough grass towards the high flat cereal plain which stretches away to the south until it touches the Wiltshire Downs.

The Terrace is a masterpiece of yews cut with precision into shapely blocks that almost form a maze. They look wonderful when the fields beyond are dank and colourless in winter, and equally good in summer when the golden wheat is high. They provide shelter, architectural interest, and private sitting places or secret temporary hideaways.

If the terrace door is open, flanked by a great tub of agapanthus and billowing mophead hydrangeas, it is possible for your eyes to pierce the massive house and glimpse that cool circle of green grass where we came in.

Mary Biddulph is a fine plantswoman (to use that clumsy word), and a gardener to her bones. She belongs to a generation inconvenienced by two World Wars and she has seen dramatic changes in the pattern of social life around her but, despite everything, her labours in the garden – with little paid help these days – reward her and her visitors with untold happiness and satisfaction.

The Topiary Garden, Rodmarton Manor

THE CHIPPING CROFT

Tetbury, Gloucestershire

The Chipping Croft (chipping – market place; croft – dwelling) sits at the bottom of the hill which runs down from the north-eastern side of the Market Square in Tetbury. Dr and Mrs Taylor came here six years ago and were met with a sea of thistles which had had the place to themselves for two growing seasons. Resplendent with Regency additions, the house is thought to date at its core from the late sixteenth century.

The bowl-shaped garden, with terraces facing the sun on the northern side, extends to about two acres. It is divided principally into large lawn, bowery walkway, natural-looking woodland, courtyard with pool, and kitchen garden above a wide terrace containing three distinct garden areas of its own.

For a short time after the Second World War the house was used as a school. Its now-redundant hard-surfaced playing ground is occupied today by a long rectangular pool raised to eighteen inches or so above the paving. Ornamental carp and water-lilies loll in still waters enlivened by the plash from two centrally-placed spouts. The gap between the two surrounding walls is filled with soil, enabling low-growing plants which require sharp drainage to thrive in a waterside setting. Clear yellow herbaceous potentillas, sunny heli-anthemums and *Stachys lanata*, tumbling over the local stone, are typical of the plants used to good effect in this part of the garden. The play of light on water can also be enjoyed from a newly-installed conservatory of elaborate design which runs along one side of the house.

At the far end of the pool wide stone steps lead strollers to the first

The gravel walk, The Chipping Croft

of two terraced levels. New Zealand flax, *Phormium tenax*, in two flanking groups, emerges spear-like from clumps of euphorbia and robust hardy geraniums. Urns filled with summer-yellow pansies light the way.

The three terrace-gardens, some six to eight feet above the pool, have been made on the site of a giant fruit cage which the Taylors inherited. Soft fruits have now been relegated to yet another, higher, level in the garden, leaving this dramatic semi-elevated site for a more exciting and, as it turns out, more romantic creation.

By dividing this area Dr Taylor has made three formally-designed gardens which, in summer, are each crowded with a wide variety of flowering and edible plants. The first garden here was intended to be mostly of white flowers, but interlopers and squatters have arranged things otherwise. The heart of this section is an elliptically-shaped lawn surrounded with masses of white *Viola cornuta* and a mixture of perennials including delphiniums and burnt bronzy-brown geums. In June the euphorbias were past their best and their massive limey seedheads were picking themselves up after having been thrown to the ground by summer showers. Where the delphiniums had been staked they remained upright and proud, others had flopped or broken; unlike the leggy foxgloves, similarly battered, they were not turning up their flower spikes again in balletic arabesques.

From the 'oval' garden into a 'circular' one whose round lawn is outlined by box plants brought from a house in Devon. These bushes will as they grow be fashioned into scalloped shapes. An octagonal reconstituted stone urn in the centre spills bright pink pelargoniums among the surrounding planting, predominantly silver foliage and pale yellow flowers.

The centre of the last of these adjoining gardens, still on the same level, is square with a pattern made of bricks laid on the soil to provide a path through the beds. Salad greens and herbs hobnob it here among cottage garden plants providing a relaxed, more homely, mood. Steps to the right lead to the kitchen garden proper where rows of leeks, onions, carrots and lettuces live happily between the asparagus bed and the new fruit cage bursting in summer with strawberries, raspberries and gooseberries. Dr Taylor's hives are sited on the wall overlooking the lower terrace gardens. His honey, for sale to callers and garden visitors alike, is much prized.

The great set-piece in this garden is the wide path directly under the terraces where hoops of roses, honeysuckles and clematis arch over a long wide path leading back to a sitting area immediately in front of the drawing-room window. Deliberately, or perhaps not, Dr Taylor has surfaced this path with granite chippings, not the more obvious Cotswold stone chippings. The colour, smokey grey on dry days and mysteriously dark in wet weather, is the perfect foil to the edging of catmint which is allowed to sprawl from both sides and touch in the middle here and there.

A large well-kept lawn, at the lowest level in the garden, spreads itself across from this pathway to a long border of the yellow and white poached-egg plants (*Limnanthes douglasii*) which provide ample nectar for the bees in the early summer months when the first rush of spring flowers is over and before the midsummer profusion gets under way. A mature belt of woodland trees beyond the lawn provides a barrier to both neighbouring houses and some of the town's unwanted noise.

The Taylors have made a bountiful garden hidden among the streets of Tetbury; it is neither a town garden in the accepted sense, nor is it a country garden remote from the bustle of suburban life. It is something of its own: a secret place, scented by flowers, humming with bees, and rich in good things for the kitchen table.

A West Highland terrier at The Chipping Croft

HIGHGROVE HOUSE

Near Tetbury, Gloucestershire

P rince Charles is as dedicated to the well-being of his garden as he is to the nation's architecture and to the world's ecological health. With hard work and no chemicals he has, in ten years at Highgrove, transformed a dozen or so flat and neglected acres into a garden of great diversity. Some parts seem happily mature already, while others are poised on the brink of fulfilment.

A beautifully planted, south-facing terrace immediately outside the drawing-room window enjoys a vista towards a wooden dovecot some distance away. In delightful contrast there is a 'cottage garden' with rose-drenched pergola and overflowing meandering borders, several acres of wild flower 'meadow', and a walled kitchen garden as productive as it is beautiful.

His Royal Highness, no stranger to working boots and toolshed, has consulted some of this country's most eminent gardeners to help him formulate his own ideas of how a garden should look. Walking with the Prince through his garden on a warm July afternoon and evening it was possible to appreciate his care for the land in general as well as his deep interest in those areas being put to the spade for ornamental or conservation purposes. Here is a romantic spirit propelled by high ideals, a love of flowers and homegrown food, tempered by an overriding concern for what looks right in the right setting.

The long vista running south is bordered by blocks of pleached hornbeams and by inner rows of mounded golden yews. Together with some magnificent, mature trees, the golden yew 'puddings' are among the very few features the Prince has preserved from the garden's previous life. But the yews are less than inspiring, and the Prince has

In the Cottage Garden, Highgrove House

plans now to let them grow and be clipped into more exciting shapes. Sir Roy Strong has helped with hedges and has worked up delightful drawings showing how swags and pompoms and Gothick windows (echoing those in a pair of pavilions on the terrace) can all be conjured from living plants to bring movement, decoration and humour into the garden. Sir Roy has even devised Prince of Wales's feathers in topiary for the secluded Rose Garden next to the house.

Informality is the key word in the Cottage Garden. With suggestions from Rosemary Verey, His Royal Highness has created a series of flowing, curving beds whose bends and turns obscure the boundaries to conjure a relaxed and soft atmosphere – a world within a world. Here, in summer, the Prince and his family are surrounded by the sounds and fragrances particular to an English country garden.

One section of the Cottage Garden has a cool ambience where *Prunus subhirtella* 'Autumnalis' with white semi-double flowers in the spring, and *Philadelphus* 'Belle Etoile' – whose fragrant white flowers follow in summer – are planted among viburnums with white foxgloves, epimediums and variegated hostas to smother any weeds. More flowering cherries and philadelphus varieties are repeated along this sweeping border, mixed well with an array of other shrubs and small trees including *Elaeagnus × ebbingei*, *Leycesteria formosa* with autumn berries beloved by pheasants, lilacs, *Cotinus coggygria* 'Royal Purple', a group of *Daphne odora* near the front so that nostrils can more easily reach its perfume, and *Magnolia × soulangiana* 'Lennei' with huge goblets of fleshy, rosy-pink-stained flowers. They are underplanted thickly with pale pink *Geranium endressii*, variegated brunneras with their forget-me-not-like blue flowers, spiky verbascums, tiarella, bergenias, polygonums and hellebores all generously distributed to flow around and between the spreading limbs of the flowering shrubs.

An opposite bed whose curves echo its partner's contours is filled largely with herbaceous plants designed to reach their peak in the summer months. Again cool colours are prominent: *Campanula persicifolia*, pale astilbes, acanthus and nepeta fill a wide stretch where the theme continues with sweet rocket and bleeding hearts, bergamot, pearly achillea, phloxes, white honesty, aquilegias and sedums. Frills of violas form a spilling edge interrupted here and there with silvery patches of *Helichrysum angustifolium*, love-in-a-mist and delicate daisies.

In the depths of the Cottage Garden roses find their way into the groups of shrubs. Next to *Prunus pollardii* is a trio of 'Stanwell Perpetual', a blush-pink, repeat-flowering Scotch rose discovered in an Essex garden and introduced to commerce in 1838 by the London nurseryman, Lee of Hammersmith. 'Amy Robsart', a form of the sweet brier, *Rosa eglanteria*, whose leaves smell of fresh green apples, is planted nearby and happily tolerates some shade. Overhead, in mature trees which have been skilfully rid of any storm-damaged boughs, ropes of wisteria are being encouraged to invade the higher reaches in a similar fashion to those at another Royal garden, the Savill, in Windsor Great Park in Berkshire.

In an interview with *The Times* (30th December, 1989) His Royal Highness said that one of the reasons he was attracted to the

Sweet pea tunnel in the Kitchen Garden, Highgrove House

Highgrove estate was 'the beautiful walled [kitchen] garden' which he found 'irresistible'. I can see why. It is approximately one acre in extent and almost square, with the twenty-foot-high brick walls now restored to their original condition. The Prince worked on the layout with the Marchioness of Salisbury, a Trustee of the Museum of Garden History in London, chronicler of the Queen Mother's gardens, and whose own garden at Hatfield House in Hertfordshire ranks among England's horticultural glories.

The Kitchen Garden is quartered, and each section is subdivided again to accommodate many ornamental features and planting schemes as well as areas for a more traditional style of vegetable growing. The four main crossing paths, meeting in a wide circle in the centre, are covered with warm-coloured pea gravel. The secondary paths are either of mown grass or paved with bricks similar to those used for the walls. Low box hedges emphasise the geometry of many of the paths but give easy access to the beds. Tunnels are made of birch and hazel sticks (from the estate) and beans and sweet peas clothe them in the summer months. Espaliered fruit trees, including a medlar, apricots, plums and cherries, fan out on the walls to benefit from the warmth held by the bricks. At their feet, enjoying the same brick-stored heat, are waves of unrestrained herbs lapping the gravel, releasing their 'southern' fragrances onto the still air. The lack of any straight lines at the feet of the walls is a wonderful example of Vita Sackville-West's notion that maximum formality of design should contain maximum *informality* of planting. How that romantic soul from Sissinghurst Castle would have loved to walk these paths. Fragrance comes also from roses, waist-high hedges of sweet briers, and 'Rosa Mundi' with flowers striped in two shades of pink.

The centre of the Kitchen Garden contains a circular pond with a tiered fountain. Around the edge a white-painted picket fence prevents the young princes from a dowsing. Surrounding the pool thymes and marjorams weave among each other, and sage, fennel and rosemary make mounds and lacy patterns. In segments there are four arcs of standard-trained 'Golden Hornet' crab apples forming a living crown or coronet.

Still within the Kitchen Garden, there are rows of apples and pears, apple and vine tunnels, quinces and cherries, all with plentiful honeysuckles for scent. Kitchen produce is also grown here in large quantities, with surpluses given to local hospitals and charitable organisations; some is taken to London where organically raised food from the country garden can be enjoyed at Kensington Palace. Any one year's crops will make a list not dissimilar to those drawn up by conscientious allotment holders throughout the land: cabbages in several varieties; leeks, carrots, Brussels sprouts, peas; runner, dwarf and broad beans; salad greens, beetroot and early-cropping potatoes. Herbs have been mentioned, but it is worth pointing out that they too are destined for the kitchen and the dining-room, and are not grown just for the fun of it, although there is almost no greater sensual pleasure in the garden than to take a broken herb leaf to your nose as you go about your rounds. There is also clipped topiary in the Kitchen Garden, and beds full of herbaceous flowering plants, and more roses, including David Austin's 'English' varieties which carry such names as 'Gertrude Jekyll', 'Heritage', 'William Shakespeare' and 'Chaucer'.

The walls of the Kitchen Garden have been embellished here and

Approaching sunset in the Kitchen Garden, Highgrove House

there with ball finials and obelisks above ogee-shaped gates painted a delicate pink to harmonise with the brick. Tall terracotta pots from Italy stand at crucial junctions disgorging colourful sprays of geraniums and fuchsias.

Even outside horticultural circles the Prince of Wales is known for his deep love of open spaces and the wild flowers familiar to us all. At Highgrove he has insisted upon bringing the countryside almost to the house walls. Around some of the outbuildings he has encouraged what Miriam Rothschild saucily calls her Farmers' Nightmare Mixture, an assortment of seeds consisting of such 'favourites' as corn-cockle, corn marigold, poppy, cornflower, May weed, a little wild barley and a few wild grasses. The Prince is pleased to see how many birds these wild and hedgerow plants bring to his garden. Miriam Rothschild has also worked with the Prince to help him make his Wild Flower Meadow. Here the Prince wanted also to include bulbs to remind him of the glorious flora of the Alps and European grasslands; he has used wild gladiolus (*G. byzantinus*), camassias, martagon lilies, Dutch, Spanish and English irises among the annual and perennial species which probably amount to over one hundred kinds. British native orchids have also been introduced (by seed) and it will be especially interesting to see if they can compete over the years with the vigorous native grasses which Highgrove's rich soil allows to grow so strongly. A similar mixture of wild flowers, combined with more Farmers' Nightmare, has been planted in a nine-foot-wide border each side of the long drive to the house. Not all the wild flowers at Highgrove have been started by bulb planting or seed scattering; primroses, cowslips and oxlips very often make far better headway if raised from seed in their own beds and transplanted into the turf as small plants. The meadow is cut after flowering, usually in mid to late summer depending on the season, and the seed is harvested for the following year.

With the Prince's passionate interest in trees it is not surprising

Doorway to the Park, Highgrove House

that he has incorporated a wood in his garden. Existing trees of good vintage gave him his starting point, and poor or declining species have been cleared to let in more light, and underplanted with smaller trees, shrubs and ground covering plants as well as more wild flowers. Foxgloves enjoy the shady conditions; so, too, *Campanula latifolia*, native to Scotland and parts of Europe and Asia. At Highgrove both blue and white forms of this bellflower have been introduced and their invasive tendency will be welcomed during the summer months when they will flower away riotously on stems up to two feet high.

There is more tree planting going on all the time. The Prince now holds the National Collection of beech (*Fagus* species) and some of these line the main drive. He has also demonstrated his concern for trees well beyond the walls of his own garden. He was responsible last year for saving old varieties of apples when the Duchy of Cornwall bought Brogdale, in Kent, thus preserving for the nation a remarkable collection of fruit trees from which breeders and collectors alike can learn and propagate.

Prince Charles has already made an outstanding contribution to English gardening at Highgrove. His dedicated and workmanlike team is fortunate to have for its inspiration a man whose 'green' consciousness plays a paramount role in the way labours are performed, and whose eyes are trained as much on the overall beauty of what is being created as on the methods by which it is achieved.

WESTONBIRT SCHOOL

Westonbirt, Gloucestershire

A number of large houses in England, and indeed elsewhere, have been turned into schools in an attempt to stave off decay or demolition. Few people can now run twenty- or thirty-bedroom buildings as private homes. In this country Stowe in Buckinghamshire, with a landscape shaped by William Kent and Thomas Bridgeman in the eighteenth century, is perhaps the best example. Even Sir Edwin Lutyens' chalky-white Marsh Court in Hampshire, built only in 1901–4 (for sale again as I write), has spent long years rocking to the yells of boisterous schoolboys.

In the Cotswolds one particular large Victorian house, built between 1868 and 1873, reverberates to the no less shrill utterances of several hundred schoolgirls.

The present house was built with more than an acknowledging glance at Wollaton Hall in Nottinghamshire, for millionaire Captain Robert Stayner Holford whose son, Sir George, the last lord of the manor, became Equerry-in-Waiting to the Prince of Wales in 1892 and remained in service until after the Prince ascended the throne as Edward VII.

Robert Holford (arboriculturist and orchid fancier) was not a man to have his ambitions hindered or simplified. He worked on a grand scale, incorporating an Italianate garden complete with balustrading and loggias, which exist to this day. Evidence of his love affair with Italy can be seen throughout the house, designed by the architect Lewis Vulliamy who by then had already masterminded the Holford's new London home, Dorchester House in Park Lane.

The estate had been in the family since an ancestral Holford married in 1665. Although this marriage produced no heir (a second marriage did) it brought into the family an Elizabethan manor house which was torn down in 1818 and replaced nearby with a Regency Gothic house in 1823 on the site of the present building.

Even before the new house was under way, Robert Holford began acquiring trees. As a young man in his early twenties he started planting his arboretum, which today holds a world-famous collection under the care of the Forestry Commission.

But we are concerning ourselves here with the *garden* at Westonbirt House, and not with the Arboretum, which lies on the other side of the main road.

When Simon Dorrell and I visited the school in early spring last year we noted sadly the number of fine mature trees which had come crashing to the ground in a series of February gales. Westonbirt and the entire Cotswolds was fortunate enough to largely escape the so-called Great Storm of 1987 – it wrought its greatest havoc further east and south – but the loss of good specimens in 1990 certainly changed the place.

The Italianate garden, with its geometric pattern of beds and walkways, was looking a little down-at-heel last spring. Weeds had established themselves in a few places where early bulbs and flowers could have bestowed a happier appearance. It is to be hoped, though, that a newly enrolled Head of Gardens will soon make his presence felt and restore this intriguing and lovingly-made historic part of the garden. Several lovely old magnolias still bloom along the wall of the Italian Garden, and looking south one can feel distant Italy, although unfortunately in the north aspect the illusion is broken by the intrusion of the roofline of a modern building above the high walls.

Other parts of the garden are very beautiful. Westonbirt House was not the only establishment in the Cotswolds to thrill us with the sight of acres of naturalised *Anemone blanda* in shades of pale blue and white. Here they grew across the distant lawns, into the wooded areas, and under and around standing and fallen trees. Daffodils in carefree clumps provided contrasting points of colour, and generous tufts of primroses added an extra sparkle.

A 1952 plan of the garden shows an outstanding number of remarkable trees in the grounds. For instance, the Mercury Garden,

In the Italianate garden, Westonbirt School

beyond the Italian Garden, so named for its little statue of the god standing in a circular pool, is surrounded by *Magnolia soulangiana*, Japanese cut-leaved maple, silver-striped hedgehog holly, *Juniperus virginiana* (the pencil cedar), Cripps' cypress (*Chamaecyparis obtusa* var. *crippsii*) and the Japanese pagoda tree (*Sophora japonica*), to name but a few. Reading the tree list is like studying an arboreal *Who's Who*; trees

167

from all over the temperate world and many natives have been planted here, and most of them survive. A meandering stroll will bring you in touch with exotic acers, uncommon firs, cedars and cypresses, a remarkably diverse collection of hollies and junipers, walnuts, magnolias, spruces and pines, unusual ash, oaks, beeches and elms, and many more broadleaf and coniferous specimens serving as an appetiser for the main arboretum nearby.

I left feeling that surely a few girls educated at Westonbirt must have been inspired to follow a career in horticulture. Later on in the summer I had the pleasure of being shewn one of the Cotswolds' finest gardens (included in this book) and learnt, to my pleasure, that its owner was indeed a Westonbirt girl.

Essex House

Badminton, Gloucestershire

If one has not gardened as a child it seems that forty is the magic age. I have met countless people, men and women, who picked up their first spade or pulled their first weed at around that time in life. So it was with Alvilde Chaplin after she inherited a house near Versailles. Later, during a long period spent domiciled in France, she moved to the Mediterranean where she was able to make a very different sort of garden from the one further north.

In 1951 Alvilde married the writer James Lees-Milne, who took her to meet his friends the Nicolsons at Sissinghurst Castle. By this time Alvilde had been thoroughly smitten by gardening. She could not fail to be 'deeply inspired' by what Vita Sackville-West and Harold Nicolson were doing in Kent, and she recalls that Vita was always immensely helpful and did not mind being asked stupid questions.

The Lees-Milnes moved to Alderley Grange near Wotton-under-Edge in 1960 and made the garden which Mr Guy and the Hon. Mrs Acloque eventually acquired in 1974.

Alvilde Lees-Milne gardens now at Essex House, an elegant, roughcast, late seventeenth-century Caroline house with an applied ochre wash, situated at the gates to Badminton House. Summer visitors are greeted with the flower-scent of Climbing 'Lady Hillingdon' rose, and the foliage-fragrance of *Rosa primula*, the incense rose, growing in shade by the north-facing front door. The narrow front garden leads to the side of the house where old box hedges and Portugal laurels line the garden walls. Almost hidden in the glossy evergreen foliage is a terracotta bust of a Caesar whose eyes seem to watch your every move.

This is not a large garden by country standards but its quarter of an acre or so is generous in a village. Three mature cedars of Lebanon once dominated the scene, but one of the 1990 February gales brought two of them crashing to the ground, doing extensive damage to garden and walls. Alvilde Lees-Milne, a women not known to dither, ensured that everything was made good again before the autumn. To her eyes, though, the garden has changed utterly. Permanent shade at one end of the plot has given way to light, entirely altering the conditions for those plants like foxgloves and cyclamen which used to revel in day-long gloaming. But on an October visit last year hundreds of cyclamen leaves were showing in the grass (at a suitable moment when one reckons to have put the mower away for six months) so it is to be hoped that they will adapt to their new invasion of sunlight. Cyclamen varieties to be found in this garden include autumn and wintering flowering *C. hederifolium*, *C. cilicium* and *C. coum* which occur in the wild from southern Italy to Asia Minor.

The crashing cedars could have been even more destructive. A marble statue of Apollo escaped decapitation by just six inches. Today he stands in a newly-made enclosure free from the threat of falling branches, cradled in an arched frame surrounded by an arc of yew and variegated hollies. Around his feet grow ivies including the variegated Canary Island ivy known as 'Gloire de Marengo', and the invasive *Euphorbia amygdaloides* var. *robbiae* which is pulled out by the handful. Over the arch are the pale roses 'Félicité et Perpétue' and 'Rose Marie Viaud'.

The stump of the largest cedar has been routed out, but a low hummock survives to mark the spot where its companion in death once stood. More foxgloves have been scattered here to create a little woodland patch under the delicate shade of three young *Betula jacquemontii* which will grow tall on their shining white stems. Pale daffodils including white *Narcissus* 'Mount Hood' and 'Beersheba', and blue *Anemone blanda* 'Atrocaerulea' bring this part of the garden into flower early in the year.

A few roses grown in the grass at the far end of the garden add a looser style of planting in contrast to the formality nearer the house. *Rosa californica* 'Plena', large-flowered 'Charles de Mills', the vigorous Gallica 'Complicata', blush-pink 'Fritz Nobis', the prolific-hep-

The bust of a Caesar, Essex House

bearing *Rosa moyesii* 'Geranium' and the early-flowering, pale yellow *R. pteragonis* 'Cantabrigiensis' – all above head height – now also find themselves with more sun to bathe in. The rose 'Albéric Barbier' with beautiful yellow buds and flowers and healthy-looking glossy foliage clothes the far fence but its heads face the sun, away from this garden towards a neighbour's plot.

The rectangular-shaped garden has another much smaller rectangle to one side on land seemingly borrowed from Badminton Park. This forms the Pond Garden, edged with borders full of spring flowers. The principal accents come from standard 'Pearl Drift' and 'Iceberg' roses – quite capable of carrying their remontant flowers well into winter – in the north and south borders. Beneath them, in the far border, are bright patches of variegated strawberry and variegated ground elder (*Aegopodium podagraria* 'Variegata', perfectly acceptable in the garden, unlike its rampant and all-invasive plain-leaved brother) and *Houttuynia cordata variegata* with heart-shaped leaves that release an aromatic smell of bitter Seville orange peel when they are crushed. Scrophularia, alliums, pale mauve double primulas, *Mahonia* × 'Charity' and a curious berberis which has sprouted boughs of both purple and green foliage, are all to be found in this border. The rigid standard 'Iceberg' roses are planted just proud of the border, like columns in front of a low arcade. The pond from which this garden takes its name is also rectangular, emphasising the strong geometry of this garden within a garden.

As late as early November there are pots of marguerite-like 'Jamaican Primrose' chrysanthemums (now clumsily labelled *Argyranthemum frutescens*) in an improbable and welcoming spring-like shade of yellow for that time of the year. In the other border are more standard 'Pearl Drift', and the roses 'Amber Queen' and 'Buff Beauty', almost equally capable of displaying late bloom, if not quite so abundantly as 'Pearl Drift' whose apple-blossom buds and flowers *do* go on and on. The screen between this part of the enclosure and the main garden is a wooden pergola where 'Madame Alfred Carrière' and Climbing 'Iceberg' disport themselves gladly.

Osmareas (now more correctly *Osmanthus* × *burkwoodii* since the taxonimists have interfered with one of its parents), bearing vanilla-scented flowers in early summer, and standard-grown variegated euonymus, line a path leading back down one side of the main garden where upright forms of *Juniperus communis* make taller, thinner statements. Where a slight change in the level occurs a narrow border crosses the garden; at the extreme left- and right-hand sides two *Pyrus salicifolia* 'Pendula' (planted for the Queen's Silver Jubilee in 1977), clipped like shaggy umbrellas, echo the larger shapes made by a pair of similarly-positioned *Amelanchier laevis* near the house. Following the 1990 drought these lost their leaves very early, foregoing their usually reliable show of rich autumn colour. Amelanchiers, like some of the smaller *Prunus* species, are among the best trees for small gardens; in addition to their autumn show they bear small, fragrant white flowers among the emerging pink-tinged leaves in May, and there are berries too which will entice birds later.

Centrally-placed steps lead directly to Apollo in his bower. The narrow border itself is thickly planted with low-growing campanulas, *Viola cornuta*, variegated forms of symphytum and vinca, white and purple alliums ('Purple Sensation' and *A. christophii*), some of the smaller hostas, anthemis and blue Jacob's ladders backed with a new hedge of yew and box mixed together.

The widest border in the garden, raised a little and edged with stone, runs for thirty feet or so, north to south on the east side of the garden. On the wall behind are many clematis, the climbing rose 'Constance Spry', abutilons, Moroccan sage, piptanthus, and ceanothus (a Californian native) which usually needs to be replaced after severe bouts of winter freezing. 'Maigold' and 'Cardinal Hume' roses occupy a space crowded with a mixture of shrubs, other climbers, perennials and annuals. Echiums and cosmos are among annuals sown recently by Mrs Lees-Milne to fill the gaps created by the crashing cedars between the shrubs, and to keep the flag flying after the perennials have bowed out. Yet another ceanothus has been planted in this border – pandering to a passion for blue flowers – and it associates well with artemisias and *Verbena* 'Silver Ann'. Tall pyrethrums, rich-purple scabious-like *Knautia macedonica* and white and pink penstemons add to the lush assortment of plants which keep this border flowering over a long period.

'Cardinal Hume' pops up again in another bed, edged with clipped box shapes, which runs parallel with the back of the house. This is a warm spot where herbaceous salvias and cistuses thrive. Here, too, Mrs Lees-Milne indulges her love for ever more roses and has planted 'Rosa Mundi', 'Petite de Hollande', 'Queen of Denmark' and thorny-stemmed 'William Lobb' whose dark crimson flowers turn to pale lavender as they die.

The centrepiece of this garden is the formal 'knot'. I asked Alvilde what she called such a prominent feature in the garden. 'I don't call it anything, I don't think it's grand enough to have a name', was her reply. Nameless perhaps, but this strong, 'architectural' feature is the overriding influence on the garden at all times of the year. The design straddles the central walkway and in the centre of each half there is a large copper urn, weathered turquoise, planted with mophead box.

In 1987 Mrs Lees-Milne wrote about her garden in *The New Englishwoman's Garden*, edited by herself and Rosemary Verey. Of this part of the garden she said: 'Fortunately when we moved here I brought quite a lot of clipped box pyramids and balls. Today they are an astronomical price and quite difficult to find. Having removed them from their tubs, I have placed them at strategic points in the garden. They also help punctuate the design of a formal arrangement in the centre of the lawn. The flagstones were already there, forming a sort of semi-circle on each side of the axial path. I edged the whole thing with box and placed pyramids symmetrically. A smaller form of box edging follows the pattern inside and the space between them is filled with *Stachys olympica,* thymes, creeping campanulas [*Campanula poscharskyana* has proved too brutish – almost as unfriendly as its name], helianthemums and various other low-growing plants and bulbs, including species tulips, chionodoxas and scillas. At the four corners of this curious arrangement I have standard hollies, *Ilex* × *altaclarensis* 'Golden King'. The hollies and the box are a joy in winter when everything else disappears or looks sad and tatty. I also think that in a small garden a certain amount of formality is necessary, so this idea is continued along the axial path which divides the lawn. On each side are six pairs of pyramids of variegated box. These took a long time to bush out, for variegated plants seem to grow more slowly.'

On the south-facing back and west-facing side of the house there is a splendid horticultural tangle of climbers including wisteria, *Vitis coignetiae, Clematis cirrhosa balearica,* and *Clematis alpina* 'Miss Bateman', *C. a.* 'Frances Rivis' and 'Perle d'Azur', ivy, golden hop, and rampant honeysuckles. The wisteria has woven its way through two French-bred roses – 'Madame Caroline Testout' and 'Gloire de Dijon' – reminders perhaps of Alvilde's youthful days in France. (Another French-sounding rose in this happy muddle, 'Madame Grégoire Staechelin', was in fact raised in Spain by the man who bred the invaluable shrub rose 'Nevada'.) This wall planting is an encouraging lesson to those reluctant gardeners shy of planting anything more than one climber to every fifteen feet of house.

There is a bed by the back of the house, raised a little and mulched with gravel, which looks like an open jewel box for much of the year. Dark-red-flowered standard honeysuckles and the ancient Jacobite rose *Rosa alba* 'Maxima', also known as the 'Great Double White' or 'Cheshire Rose', rise above white and pale blue pulmonarias, multitudes of small bulbs, *Potentilla vilmorinii*, blue linum (flax), *Euphorbia amygdaloides* 'Rubra' and *E. cyparissias*, low-growing hardy herbaceous geraniums and *Ceratostigma willmottianum* from western China which bears its intensely-blue flowers just as the foliage takes on a burnished, burgundy glow.

Alvilde Lees-Milne still travels extensively in France. She under-

The formal garden, Essex House

takes garden planning there as well as in this country. At present she is making a large garden for Mick Jagger in the Loire Valley and a much smaller one for Madame Giscard d'Estaing nearby. I cannot say that I detect a French influence in her own garden – perhaps none exists – but it is clear that the maker of this garden has brought with her an understanding of gardening traditions from more than one country and from more than one period. When the summer and autumn flowers have gone, when the last leaf has fallen, still there will be the pleasing shapes of the clipped low hedges and boxwood pyramids in tunics of glassy frost. And hidden among the twigs and stems of dormant shrubs and roses the frail-looking but thoroughly tough little hellebores and cyclamen will be having a party all of their own.

INTERLUDE

IV

Beverston Castle – Beverston, Gloucestershire
Hodges Barn – Shipton Moyne, Gloucestershire
Badminton House – Badminton, Gloucestershire
Hill House – Wickwar, Gloucestershire

Here in the southern reaches of the Cotswolds there is a marked change in the lie of the land; the steep-sided valleys give way to level prairie-like pasture from Tetbury to Badminton. We are on our southern boundary; to the west, at Wickwar, we are on the foothills of the escarpment which properly defines the Cotswolds' western limit.

Simon Dorrell and I visited the garden at BEVERSTON CASTLE in March. The hamlet crouches low among large fields and is dominated by the keep of the thirteenth-century Castle. Not sure of our directions, we followed our noses down a narrow lane bounded by random-stone walls and found ourselves skirting the massive tower to discover the church, dwarfed by its protective neighbour – the strong defending the meek. We parked by the lych-gate and strolled down to what we believed to be the gatehouse. Sunshine sliced through the lazy smoke of a damp bonfire. A dog barked; I would like to think a horse neighed. Who, in this remarkable atmosphere – a survival of medieval England – could fail to make a romantic garden?

Shrubs cling to the walls of an inner courtyard of the house, which occupies the site of the old banqueting chamber. A stone trough is filled with red tulips open widely to the early sunshine.

The south-facing terrace of the house must be among the most

Pulsatilla vulgaris on the terrace, Beverston Castle

beautifully planted areas of paving in the country. With the tower of
the castle dominating one end Mrs Rook, whose garden this is, has
taken full advantage of the warm and sunny aspect. The wisteria and
rose stems on the house ripen well each year to ensure the following
summer's profusion of blooms. At their feet are billowing euphorbias,
and crown imperials add splashes of early colour. Among the paving
cracks many low-growing, and surprisingly non-low-growing, plants
have been encouraged to spread in all directions. Many thymes,
pasque flowers, campanulas, small hardy geraniums, alchemilla and
sisyrinchiums are typical of those individuals which have seeded
themselves between and under shrubs. Scent is trapped by the high
walls; at the height of the season it is almost impossible to tread the
stone without damaging any of the profusely scattered plants. The
terrace is linked to the garden by a bridge over a dry moat where

climbing plants have been allowed to hang in great swags. Railings along the bridge prevent a nasty fall.

In springtime paths will be cut through the narcissi-studded grass out among trees, leading to flower borders in outlying parts of the main garden.

HODGES BARN rises like an apparition over fields on the Shipton Moyne-to-Malmesbury road. Its extraordinary outline – with two fascinating domes – sets it apart from any other agricultural building. It serves no farming purpose, nor has it since 1939 when, some four hundred years after being built, it was converted into an unusual house occupied today by Mr and Mrs Hornby. The garden surrounds the building on all sides.

At Hodges Barn two abiding principles of good garden design have been observed. First, those areas dominated by the house itself

Spring, Hodges Barn

respond respectfully to the architecture. From the front of the house the eye is led across a small courtyard, up stone steps past companion pieces of fine and rather eccentric topiary, between elegant carved stone pineapples to a large raised lawn whose presence is announced by four upright Irish yews. When one looks back two tapestry hedges, like theatre curtains drawn apart, reveal stage flats before a fanciful backdrop – the house itself. The scene is set.

Act Two, so to speak, is played out on the other side of the house. Double doors open onto a generous stage where steps planted with aubrietia might induce the players' flight from the boards between ball-capped piers into the countryside. This formal treatment enhances the house, and ennobles the landscape beyond.

The second principle observed follows on from the first: as the presence of the house is diminished by distance, so should its influence upon design be less apparent. On a spring morning in bright sunshine the informal gardens to the east of the house were dancing with daffodils in a cast of thousands. In large troupes the narcissi scented the crisp air and exhilarated our senses. Randomly they appeared over several acres around a large pond and beneath tall trees whose first leaves were just emerging.

When the time comes to change the cast, the summer season will bring on the roses – climbing, billowing and tumbling.

'BADMINTON has always been the grandest seat in Gloucestershire. With its vast estates it is still a sort of principality, still with a reigning duke. Yet there is an unaccountable homeliness about it.' So begins James Lees-Milne's chapter on Badminton House in *Some Cotswold Country Houses*. We have looked over the garden walls of Essex House (in the village of Badminton) to see James and Alvilde Lees-Milne's own garden; now we catch a glimpse of the garden world beyond the high gates of the 'big house'.

Let us stay with James Lees-Milne as he describes the surrounding land:

Evidently the 1st Duke's chief concern was his park. The terrain being pancake flat enabled him to work on a gigantic scale. He made the house the nucleus of thirty straight rides which were intersected by some 24 others radiating from the *rond-point* to the south-east. Although William Kent designed 'an improvement on Ye Lawn' in 1745 and Capability Brown was paid in 1752 for plans for various landscape alterations, all of which came to nothing, the lesser known Thomas Wright of Durham left a more positive impression on the surroundings of Badminton. He too made a number of landscape suggestions which again were ignored, but he did carry out several ornamental park buildings. The 1st Duke's network of rides was smudged by time's inexorable change rather than by the positive hands of improvers. Yet several of his straight rides can still be traced, notably that great survivor, the drive from the north entrance of the house to Worcester Lodge, the east avenue and Centre Walk (actually just off-centre) which stretches obliquely from the south front across the railway and even beyond the M4 motorway [some three or four miles distant].

One of this garden's other remarkable sights today occurs very early in the year, in February usually. *Crocus tomasinianus,* in shades of pale blue and violet with occasional white flowers to lighten the effect, are

Hornbeam, Badminton House

scattered widely under oaks and spreading cedars. They have naturalised over the years to form tight patches between which it would now
be almost impossible to plant another bulb. They glow on dreary days
in late winter, but when the first spring sunshine comes they reflect
bright shields of light onto the undersides of overhanging branches:
signals of better days coming.

The main part of the garden at Badminton House lies at the back
(south) embraced by a projecting wing of the house, stables and the
church. The 'open' side has been screened by hornbeam hedges to
create a large, enclosed garden with fountains and wide borders of
many old roses and herbaceous plants. Caroline Somerset, the present
Duchess of Beaufort, comes to Badminton House having earned her
gardening laurels at the Dower House outside the gates. She
has added new formal enclosures and knot gardens and in
recent times work has begun to revive the old walled Kitchen
Garden.

Sally, Duchess of Westminster died while we were making our
observations for this book. At the turn of the year HILL HOUSE, her
home for many years, was still for sale. The future of her beguiling and
indiosyncratic garden remains in doubt.

The Duchess returned to Gloucestershire from Cheshire in 1970 –
she and the Duke of Westminster had formerly lived at Didmarton. At
Hill House she was presented with roughly seven acres of flat land to
shape and fashion as she chose. Part was fenced off as grazing land for
her flock of black Welsh mountain sheep.

Sally was a great traveller and her home was full of rugs and *objets*
brought back from the countless wanderings to which she was so
addicted – almost to the time of her death. In some ways her garden
reflected magpie instincts, too, and over the years she began collections of numerous groups of plants. There were hollies, an interest she
shared with Mary Biddulph at Rodmarton Manor; and her especial
love: plants with gold and silver foliage.

A touch of exotica permeated the garden with the squawks from a
large aviary of colourful birds (now safely rehomed) and one can only
assume that their view over a garden full of strange and lovely plants
allowed them to keep at least one claw on the perch of sanity.

Rose hoops, Hill House

Flat gardens are often described as being the poorer for not enjoying a variety of levels. At Hill House this possible problem was solved by siting large trees quite close to the house so that there is no immediate view of a smooth and disappearing landscape.

Sally introduced only one formal element, pleaching a row of limes near the aviary to make a walk flanked by wide borders of shrubs and herbaceous perennials. She found exisiting copper beech, blue Atlantic cedar and *Tilia petiolaris*. The terrace is sheltered by a large yew and a weeping larch which stand each side of a small pond where willow, juniper and purple-leaved hazel add to the crowded effect. The rose 'New Dawn' flourishes on a sunny corner of the house at a point where paths disappear in two directions. One leads under a black mulberry to the vegetable borders beside a boundary wall near hellebores thickly planted in shady beds under birch, cherries and ornamental acers. A hint of mystery was once evoked by a row of four Florentine

183

columns beside a second blue Atlantic cedar, but these had disappeared by the time I made my last visit in December when I went to dig some plants for Sally's sister who has a small London garden.

Medium-sized trees play a prominent role at Hill House; there are more yews and birches and flowering cherries, another black mulberry, *Parrotia persica, Cercidiphyllum japonicum, Koelreuteria paniculata* (said to be the spreading tree on Willow Pattern china) and *Acer platanoides* 'Goldsworth Purple'. There are enough evergreen trees for the garden not to appear transparent in winter, and in shrub or tree or on the ground something could usually be found in flower at any time of the year.

The rose tunnel is fashioned out of iron hoops and although it is not particularly long, its length is exaggerated by the fact that its serpentine path obscures the end; you might be embarking upon a long meandering stroll. At some distance from the house, near the

The house, above a clamour of daisies, Hill House

sheepfold, is a small paved area with a statue ringed by low-growing plants including herbs.

In front of the house there is a separate garden which falls away among closely-planted trees. Here the grass was cut less often and its sinuous pathways took you through tunnels of dappled sunlight imbued with that enigmatic smell which emanates from damp and leafy places.

Sally was still buying plants up to a few weeks before she died. She would hear of an irresistible plant from someone, her neighbour Keith Steadman perhaps, and track it down ruthlessly. On other occasions she would be smitten by a plant in a nursery, buy it and only decide upon where to place it when she returned to her garden. Enthusiastic plant collecting on this scale is fascinating to watch. The results can be aesthetically bankrupting, but not at Hill House. While no strong claims could be made for the excellence of the overall design, the garden did have (and still has, I hope) the unique feel of a place fashioned by the heart, not the head. Gardens cannot last forever, but let us hope that Sally's curious creation survives for a while as a memorial to a remarkable lady.

KEITH STEADMAN, ESQ

WESTEND HOUSE

Wickwar, Gloucestershire

K eith Steadman is one of that small privileged group of people one supposes to have achieved what he set out to do in his garden. In a little over three acres he has developed a jungle of exciting plants, grown to a density that could only have been imagined in the man's eye when, forty years ago, he began planting-schemes on a tract of land to the south and west of his large house.

Two copper beeches marked the entrance then, and their companions were a solitary holm oak (*Quercus ilex*) and a cedar of Lebanon; they sailed over an ocean of brambles like stately tall ships blown off course. Today the copper beeches still stand but the brambles have ebbed to make way for a collection of rare and interesting trees and shrubs from around the world.

As you approach the house it is difficult to decide exactly what form it takes, or of what materials it is built, for it is almost completely hidden in summer behind a 'seedling' rose which in only four years has nearly engulfed the long façade. This prolific rose, allowed to behave as it would in a natural environment, typifies Mr Steadman's approach to gardening: plants are left to scramble about the place from the nearest doorstep to the furthest corner of the garden in splendid rollicking disorder.

The garden is threaded with paths of grass or ivy or other so-called ground cover plants. At his mature age (with only a few hours' help on Sunday afternoons) Mr Steadman reins in the full flagrant will of nature from the seat of his sit-on mower. It is not what most garden writers or designers would describe or recognise as 'labour-saving' gardening, but that's exactly what it is.

A seat in a glade, Westend House

A principal ambition of Mr Steadman's was to create 'treescapes', and this he has managed with originality and distinction. Soft greys billow over thick mounds of yellow (white poplars towering above golden robinia foliage), thickly underplanted with shrubs of lesser stature stretching down to touch the earth. Roses seem to lace their intriguing and inquisitive way through all this, holding everything together.

Foliage here is paramount; Mr Steadman enjoys repeating a comment he once overheard a lady make to her companion on an open day: 'My dear, this is the first garden I've ever visited where there are no flowers'.

But blossom drenches this garden, quietly, with glorious subtle effect. The roses which Keith Steadman has allowed to flourish are mostly white or in shades of pale yellow. A chance seedling with good greyish foliage was early recognised and propagated. Named 'Wickwar', it has found a safe niche in a number of catalogues, but throughout the Cotswolds its siblings can also be seen, proudly exalted as being from Mr Steadman himself. Another rose which revels in this garden was 'found' by Keith Steadman in nearby Stroud. No one seemed able to identify it, so he has named it after the owner in whose garden he spotted it. 'Mrs Honey Dyson' is a lovely name, and curiously descriptive too as the flowers are a pale buff to apricot.

The soft meandering paths throughout this garden lead a visitor ever onwards through dark tunnels to unexpected glades, and to colonies of plants in happy isolation. In one clearing an ironwork gazebo has been constructed from the panels of a balcony of a house near Bath which, twenty years ago, was under the demolition-man's hammer. Today it is enshrined within scrolling *Rosa moysii* and 'Rambling Rector', looking as if it has sat there for a hundred years.

The circuitous walks are full of botanical and horticultural surprises. By their abundance or unlikely *placement*, plants not particularly noticeable as single specimens grab your attention. The tall onion, *Allium siculum* (now *Nectaroscordum siculum*), does this very well. Its muted colours would hardly pull anyone aside when grown singly, but found in clumps many feet wide, and over three feet high, they call rightful attention to themselves when encountered on a woodland stroll.

Giant hogweed (*Heracleum mantegazzianum*) punctuates this garden all over. It self-seeds freely, and certain well-placed individual plants are left to grow to their full twelve to sixteen feet in height and stand stiffly about adding valuable accents among other more lax and graceful plantings.

Shortly after retiring from his work Mr Steadman began a small nursery to raise in modest quantity the plants he liked or which he considered difficult or rare. That phase of his life has now passed, too, but plants from that enterprise can still be found in this and other gardens. The nursery site is today a secret garden, hidden within a garden which could itself be so described.

Not all of Keith Steadman's gardening has been carried out under the shade of his lofty treescapes. At the back of the house, frocked in rampant Virginia creeper, there is a formal garden whose edges now have been blurred but whose plan still conveys a visitor along a prescribed route bulging with magnificent, fully-grown and sometimes rare shrubs. Spilling over the wide grass paths are phlomis, fennel, cistuses and a member of the only shrubby umbellifer, *Bupleurum fruticosum*, all sure reminders of the terrain around a house which Mr Steadman once occupied in the south of France.

A marvellous contrast of foliage is found in the jostling plants of *Cotinus coggygria purpureus* and the arresting glaucous leaves and stems of *Berberis temolaica*. Crowded in the old borders in this part of the garden, almost overwhelmingly, is a profusion of plants whose overall effect it would be worth travelling far to see. *Buddleia alternifolia*, rugosa roses, variegated cornus, shrubby potentillas, and creamy spikes of sisyrinchium, pushing through cushions of hypericum, all vie with each other for space and attention.

On the south-facing terrace massed euphorbias deny access to two Victorian ironwork fern-leaf benches which seem under attack also from an army of wiry cotoneasters. The overall fragrance is powerful yet ambiguous. Is it the fennel, the rampaging tarragon, the torn leaves of *Choisya ternata*, or the perfume from distant roses carried through the overhead branches on a light breeze? It is of course all these plants together, and more. This is a garden full of extraordinary pleasures rare in today's world of neatness: it is fragile, exhilarating, abundant, but above all, soothing.

The house, from the formal garden, Westend House

STANCOMBE PARK

Near Dursley, Gloucestershire

Stancombe Park leans on the Cotswold escarpment with south and westerly views over the Vale of Berkeley to the River Severn. It consists of a beautiful, four-square Georgian house, a farm, and a pleasure garden which has been almost continually worked at since the 1820s. Influences on Gerda Barlow, names from post-war years, have included Lanning Roper, Peter Coats (who died last year) and Fred Whitsey, whose regular Saturday columns in the *Daily Telegraph* continue to keep a nation of gardeners on their toes and well-informed.

Sitting in the new conservatory at Stancombe, with Gerda pouring tea from a large silver kettle and offering a party of us her thin savoury sandwiches and her delicious but almost impossibly rich *Sachertorte*, it was easy to imagine for a moment that we were all enjoying ourselves somewhere else; had we been magicked for a happy hour or so to somewhere more Continental, to Gerda's homeland perhaps, beyond the Alps? Outside, despite an array of exotic plants, there was no mistaking that this was indeed England's 'green and pleasant'.

The courtyard on the west side of the house has its former stable walls draped in climbing roses, and in square tubs tall standard-grown 'Iceberg' roses have a cooling effect in the late afternoon sun.

The main garden seems almost detached from the house. In front of the south façade of the building there is a great bowl, rather like an amphitheatre, scooped from the hillside. On the far side, on almost flat ground, the garden really begins.

Trees dominate the landscape. Old cedars blend with native broadleaves to produce the unmistakable park-like effect. Gerda

Steps to the courtyard, Stancombe Park

Barlow is herself a dendrologist and has travelled widely to pursue her knowledge. One of her recent interests is in *Cornus* species – shrubs and trees from around the temperate world – and a bank once littered with dreary laurels is now being established at Stancombe with a good collection. Some dogwoods, or cornels as they are also known, are grown for the lively winter colour of their bark; some for their leaves, which may be plain or variegated with good autumn colour too; another group has showy bracts surrounding small, insignificant flowers.

'When planting, one aims to create compositions with form, colour and texture. It is not unlike a painting. If you have a view, which must be considered for an overall pleasing effect, it should not be spoilt by an elaborate and colourful planting, for this draws the eye away from the whole picture. The planting must mould into the countryside and echo the lovely folds of the land.' Mrs Barlow wrote these words just a few years ago; she has practised what she preached, and where the land rolls away to lose itself under wooded hills there is little at that point in the garden to prevent your eye from making the escape. But where a view does not exist, or where it has been planted out, there is plenty of scope for fun and riotous colour with all sorts of planting schemes. One of the features which the Barlows inherited at Stancombe was a pair of level herbaceous borders separated by a wide grass path. A seat is poised at one end between a couple of young *Catalpa bignonioides* 'Aurea' and two almost columnar *Populus candicans* 'Aurora'. These look dramatic against the tall dark coniferous trees which not only bring the vista to such an effective stop but act as a barrier against marauding gales.

One often hears criticism today of the manner in which white paint is used in the garden, particularly on seats and benches. Here at Stancombe there is some white-painted fencing used to mark out another part of the garden where many roses grow. It looks perfectly right in this garden, and with the pale-flowering shrubs, and the silver-leaved trees, it would be difficult to convince anyone that it has been mistakenly applied.

One of my favourite parts of the 'top' garden is the roundel of *Acer pseudoplatanus* 'Worleei', the golden sycamore, which itself encircles a round of clipped golden box where live globes of clipped yellow privet and an imposing marble urn, rising above head height, with clematis scrambling about its plinth.

Gerda Barlow's interest in trees does not override everything else. She adores roses, and is passionate about a galaxy of perennial plants. She loves foxgloves, too, and plants them all over in white and shades of apricot. And with three lakes to dress she is able to indulge her delight in that vast number of plants which insist upon having at least their toes in water. Three lakes there are, indeed, but what are three lakes doing in the bowl of a Cotswold garden on a sliding escarpment? The answer is one of Gloucestershire's most romantic landscape surprises.

It seems that in the early to mid nineteenth century the then owner of Stancombe contrived to build for himself a water garden with follies and secret places. Some legends suggest that the mysterious figure was a Revd David Edwards who wanted to deceive his wife and carry on a liaison with another woman far from the marital home. Some sources claim that the wife was of 'ample proportions', which is why the maker of this garden caused his secret tunnels to be wide enough for only the most lithesome of bodies to pass through. Basil Barlow led our jolly party through the tunnel, and I am pleased to report that we all made it easily although one or two of us perhaps had to 'think thin', or turn sideways. At one moment there is a narrow window with its sill appearing to rest at water level, providing a crocodile's-eye view over

The house, Stancombe Park

A view across the lake, Stancombe Park

the sheet of water. And crocodile is a suitable metaphor, because Basil Barlow has tethered a fake one in the big lake which might just frighten off unwanted interlopers intent upon a summer dip.

Around the lake the Barlows have planted a great number of trees: willows, liquidambar, *Metasequoia glyptostroboides*, and some interesting ornamental acers which will add their own particular tones to the autumn display of turning leaves. Lacecap hydrangeas fill in well under the trees and grow contentedly in the rich soil with primulas and giant-leaved gunneras. There is a romantic, Grecian-style pavilion dating from the same period as the house, and several other whimsical buildings – one with thick glass in tiny diamond-shaped panes forming its walls as if it were a rustic greenhouse. Evelyn Waugh once lived nearby, and he is thought to have written a chunk of *Brideshead Revisited* beside the lake.

Throughout this garden there is interest from good plants in great quantity. New borders are still being made and more yew hedges have recently been planted. At Stancombe you need to make a mental gear-change between the two distinct parts; the Barlows do this with

194

ease and are able to adapt readily to wherever work needs to be done. It may be the gathering of trugsful of delicate, scented flowers one moment, and squelching in mud the next to rip out some infesting *Petasites japonicus* which spreads around the wetter parts of the garden with wild abandon. Like the two halves of a well-balanced psyche, Stancombe forms a complete and satisfying whole.

MR AND MRS KEITH MARSHALL

HUNTS COURT

North Nibley, Gloucestershire

In a little over twenty years Keith Marshall has remodelled a working dairy farm into a mature, yet still-growing, garden and nursery. He first welcomed the public nine years ago, and set up the nursery four years later. The old cattle sheds provide ideal quarters for the nuts-and-bolts part of the business, while the garden wanders out from two sides of the five-hundred-year-old farmhouse in sight of the Tyndale Monument, erected in 1866 to commemorate North Nibley's famous son, William Tyndale, born here in 1484. With the origin of roses stretching back to and beyond biblical times, it seems appropriate that these few acres should yield old and new varieties so magnificently, directly under a monument which recalls the man who first translated the Bible into English and initiated the earliest printing of a vernacular New Testament in this country.

Keith Marshall dug his first rose bed in 1976 and some of his original plants, the semi-double *Rosa californica* 'Plena' and the then recently-bred 'Nozomi', stand witness to his continued endeavours. The inhabitants of this long bed grow to well over head height and provide an impressive yet thoroughly informal entrance to Hunts Court. On the other side of the gravel drive, seemingly falling out of a low dry-stone wall, is an inspired grouping of glorious roses in graded pinks, including 'Ballerina', 'Felicia' and David Austin's deservedly-famous 'Constance Spry'. Disappearing behind this group is a path which allows the visitor to penetrate the garden proper and explore the casual abundance of roses grown as bushes in grass, up trees, and scrambling over rustic fences and a thirty-foot-long pergola.

A remarkable sight here is the sun glowing richly through the

The house, from the rose garden, Hunts Court

prominent thorns of *Rosa sericea pteracantha*, inhibiting anything but a momentary pause to admire the suit of armour for which this species is principally grown. A nearby pear tree hosts two cluster roses, the seemingly hardy and strong-growing 'Wedding Day' (keenly sought in the nursery as a popular gift for anniversaries) and 'La Mortola', the pure white selected form of *Rosa brunonii* brought to England in 1954 from the famed Hanbury garden on the Italian coast near the French border.

The pergola, which allows a long view from a rusticated summer-house to the farmhouse, is planted with a rich assortment of familiar and lesser-known roses including the fruity-scented 'May Queen', the repeat-flowering Moss 'Alfred de Dalmas' (often listed in catalogues as 'Mousseline'), the Alba 'Belle Amour' with its myrrh fragrance, and 'New Dawn', the first rose ever to receive a patent. Towards the far end, nearest the house, are 'Sanders' White', the most powerfully-scented of the Ramblers, 'The Garland', 'Madame Alfred Carrière', described by the rosarian David Austin as a white Climbing Rose without rival, 'Paul's Lemon Pillar' and the vigorous 'Claire Jacquier' with her rich yellow petals paling almost to cream with age.

The pergola itself seems to be embowered in an even greater construction, surrounded as it is with more old fruit trees supporting well-grown specimens of 'Paul's Himalayan Musk', 'Veilchenblau' and the similarly purplish but unscented Rambler 'Violette'.

Although roses are Mr Marshall's first love, his garden is planted thickly with a great many other shrubs and true perennials. One of the great sights in early summer is the row of peonies flowering away heartily in long grass. They may seem abandoned and unloved, but this is not so; it is just one of the many ways in which Mr Marshall has allowed a free hand to surprise and delight.

Keith Marshall's new-found fondness for shrubby potentillas has led him to establish an important collection which he grows throughout the garden and in a display bed of their own. It is here possible to spot the sometimes small but essential differences which past and modern-day breeders have recognised, valued and gone on to label as rediscovered or entirely new varieties. A good example of the latter is 'Wessex Silver', a form of the excellent 'Primrose Beauty' selected by Wilf Simms, a friend and expert on Middle Eastern plants.

A mown path, Hunts Court

The newcomer has paler yellow flowers than its parents and a greyer, more silvery distinction to its foliage.

Keith's wife Margaret is building a collection of penstemons and hardy geraniums, and these also find their way into beds throughout the garden. This is a large group of plants, surprisingly hardy in most cases, and just about perfect, with pinks and catmint, to grow at the feet of roses.

Before you reach the nursery, by which time you will have a long mental (or better yet, pencilled) note of things to buy, there is a formal area consisting of four beds given height with rustic poles for yet more roses. The geraniums and pinks, lavender and campanulas, tie together great mounds of shrub roses and other, taller, types. Their names roll out as a celebration of rose breeders from many countries and many decades: 'Katharina Zeimet' from Germany; 'Alister Stella Gray' raised in Somerset and known as 'Golden Rambler' in America; 'Sophie's Perpetual' found and named by the late Humphrey Brooke in Essex; 'Tour de Malakoff' from Luxemburg; 'Rose du Roi' and 'Lady Waterlow' from France; and 'Heritage', bred near Wolverhampton as recently as 1984.

During last autumn Keith and Margaret, with the help of their only full-time helper, Peter Thornhill, made a new Sundial Garden with four diagonal gravel paths crossing in the centre. A circular path links the straight ones dividing the area into eight beds. Only a few roses have been used in the centre: 'Fair Bianca', 'Katharina Zeimet', 'James Veitch' and the interesting 'Sanguinea' or 'Miss Lowe's Rose' which is thought to have originated in China and was brought into

199

cultivation in the 1880s. In two of the centre segments Margaret Marshall has installed her penstemon collection among other mainly herbaceous plants including more geraniums, campanulas, parahebes and quantities of pinks. The other beds are largely filled with shrubs, and of course more roses. Many of the shrubs are unfamiliar and it is to be hoped that as time goes on their siblings will be propagated and made available in the nursery. Among the rarer species are *Hymenanthera crassifolia*, a woody, evergreen member of the violet family; *Abeliophyllum distichum*, a fully-hardy deciduous shrub with tiny star-like, fragrant flowers in late winter; *Drimys lanceolata*, another evergreen, not reliably hardy but worth trying for its sweet-smelling flowers in April and May; and *Raphiolepsis umbellata*, evergreen again, with terminal clusters of less-obviously fragrant flowers in June. The full list is impressively long.

Keith and Margaret Marshall are dedicated to their garden; they love the work and they enjoy meeting their visitors and taking time to talk to them in the garden or advise them in the nursery: 'yes, 'Kiftsgate' *is* too large for an apple tree'. Their interests are wide, extending far beyond roses; their nursery catalogue and occasional supplements demonstrate good taste and huge variety, while the sales area is well stocked with home-propagated and a few bought-in plants.

NEWARK PARK

Ozleworth, Gloucestershire

'We're not really gardeners; we only play at it.' These unlikely words were spoken by Michael Claydon as he led us from the grassy south-facing terrace in front of the four-storey house into depths of tiered woodland planting. The 'we' consists of Robert Parsons, the National Trust tenant, and the author of this remark, his hard-working and enthusiastic helper these past half-dozen years.

Newark Park is today principally a woodland garden with massed winter aconites and snowdrops studding the grass to the west of the house as early as February. Before they begin to fade their successors, our native daffodil (*Narcissus pseudonarcissus*) and enlarging patches of naturalising violets, are making their presence known. There are cyclamen, too.

Robert Parsons is an American in love with this country's history. He 'took on' Newark in 1970 when both house and garden had been much neglected. The National Trust acquired the property in 1949 from Mrs C. A. Power Clutterbuck whose family came here in the late eighteenth century. Mr Parsons has caused sleepy lids to open by working painstakingly to restore the house and wooded acres. Here, you feel, is a private domain, lovingly tended and, more importantly, still being added to.

The house, sixteenth-century in origin, overlooks some of England's most naturally-romantic landscape. Fold unfolds beyond fold. The landscape sighs contentedly away to the distance where by day the Hawkesbury tower stands proud on the edge of the Cotswold escarpment. At night the brutal glow of orange halogen light from Bristol reflects on the underbelly of billowing clouds to remind us of

A gateway, Newark Park

man's sure 'progress'. But below the precipitously poised house a garden hides from the modern world. On a series of informal terraces winding in no seemingly planned way, through mists of pungent wild garlic in April, a path takes visitors on a woodland walk to the lake below the old carriage drive. This drive is not used now but in centuries past it brought visitors up from Ozleworth Bottom allowing them glimpses of the great house through high beeches, elms and oaks. Below the carriage drive a crinkle-crankle wall recently built by Mr Parsons forms an original-looking north boundary of a slope running down to the lake. This grassed area is gradually being put to use as a kitchen garden. The shelter will doubtless encourage early vegetables for the house, while ripening fruits will provide luscious morsels for summer eating.

A brick-built, eighteenth-century orangery with ogee windows, beside the lake, adds a further romantic element to this landscape. But why brick in a land renowned for its plentiful stone? 'For warmth', says Michael Claydon, recalling other kitchen gardens in the Cotswolds made of stone but lined with brick. And a brick wall runs out from the orangery where apricots and peaches once ripened. Mr Parsons has built his crinkle-crankle wall of brick, too, intending perhaps to plant more fruit-bearing trees that will welcome the heat. This wall is interrupted by a lean-to greenhouse whose brick arches Mr Parsons built himself. Following along from this point the stroller can emerge again into woodland and begin a steady climb up banks of wild flowers to a fort-like folly. But we are not in the real world; the folly is not an ancient remnant but a trick, again convincingly contrived by Mr Parsons who built this 'fort' where an eighteenth-century folly once stood to mark the entrance from the carriage drive into the garden. The 'newness' of the stone alone gives the game away, but that will age soon, allowing the structure to slip into the rest of the garden's sense of timelessness.

Climb now back to the house and the level areas to its west and north which look so lively in the spring with flowering bulbs. Directly behind the house is a redundant croquet lawn not yet invaded by the seeding snowdrops, crocuses and daffodils which proliferate nearby.

The fort alongside the drive, Newark Park

The orangery, beside the lake, Newark Park

Walk a little further to complete the circle to where where you began and you will enter a formal area partitioned with clipped evergreen *Lonicera nitida* planted and shaped since 1970. An apple tunnel then directs visitors back to the real world.

In this circuitous route, something has been kept from visitors' eyes. Enclosed by a head-high wall leading out from the original entrance porch of the house, and by another similarly high wall on the south elevation, lies a small formal garden spread out like an apron before the sixteenth-century east front. A sundial marks the cross-axes, whose four bordering beds hold mixed herbaceous planting to enrich and extend the garden's interest into summer. In June fiercely hot-coloured oriental poppies dominate this part of the garden. From over the wall the melancholy screech of peacocks can be heard.

In the autumn the landscape itself provides the colour. Deciduous trees stretch warm shades of red and yellow far across the dipping valley.

On days when the house is open it is possible to climb the

ladder-like stairs from the fourth floor onto the roof and survey from the castellations a piece of ancient landscape that is, quite simply, unrivalled.

A duck emerging from beneath
Pyrus salicifolia 'Pendula', Newark Park

ALDERLEY GRANGE

Alderley, Gloucestershire

H ere is passion. Here is romance. Here are strange and piquant scents riding mysteriously on the air. Guy Acloque darts about his garden like a seventeenth-century alchemist tugging at a leaf here, a piece of bark there, or a dark rose hidden beneath the skirts of a trimmed hedge in a distant corner. The end of his nose is as likely as not to be dusted with saffron-coloured pollen as he withdraws from the trumpet of a regal lily, or sighs with pleasure at the perfume let loose by the exotic incense plant (*Humea elegans*). With boyish enthusiasm this man will chant the names and point to specimens of as many rare and exotic herbs and aromatic plants as one is likely to encounter in a single private garden anywhere in the British Isles.

Alderley Grange was built in 1608 and remodelled in 1810. It has had connections with good gardeners before the present owners came here in the mid 1970s: before moving to the village of Badminton, this was James and Alvilde Lees-Milne's home, and it was occupied between 1867 and 1894 by the oriental scholar and botanist Brian Houghton Hodgson whose name is remembered by *Rhododendron hodgsonii*. During his time at Alderley Grange Hodgson was visited by several eminent Victorians including T. H. Huxley, and Sir Joseph Dalton Hooker who had succeeded his father as Director of the Royal Botanic Gardens, Kew. The botanical artist Marianne North, also connected with Kew where hundreds of her paintings are housed in the North Gallery, lived in the village.

It is principally Mrs Lees-Milne's layout that we see today, and it is extraordinary that Guy Acloque should not only have preserved the

Woad, Alderley Grange

bulk of his predecessor's plan but has continued to fine-tune it so sympathetically to his own needs and desires.

The Acloques inherited not only a beautifully designed garden but also its gardener, German-born Gunter Müller who has now been turning Alderley Grange soil for the last twenty years.

A journey through this garden is rather like exploring a set of those Russian or Chinese boxes which live inside each other in descending order of size. You enter by a great sweep next to lawn, with cistuses and roses planted straight into the gravel under the windows of the house, and the journey round the garden ends in a tight corner packed with many of the garden's treasures.

By taking the side route round the house to the main part of the garden you pass a small almost enclosed courtyard area filled with white 'Iceberg' roses edged with lavender and clipped box balls – one of Alvilde Lees-Milne's lasting fingerprints. You emerge then into a large square of lawn with a good high wall running along the southern boundary screening off the road. It is planted with dozens of climbing roses, clematis and those true-blue Californian lilacs, *Ceanothus* species. At the far end is an unusual old gazebo with an arched roof, set askew where two walls form a right angle. So romantic is it as a piece of garden architecture that it might have drifted in from the set of a Mozart opera; in fact, this part of the garden could delightfully accommodate an outdoor performance of *Così fan tutte* with the two diaphanously-clad heroines calling to their lovers from bowery walls and from behind shrubs laced with flowering tendrils.

There are splendid trees set about the grass including a magnolia and a dignified old Indian bean tree, *Catalpa bignonioides* – planted by Hodgson – which has now reached stately proportions. (The 'Indian' refers to North American Indians. Catalpas were introduced to Britain in 1726; specimens can be seen in a number of Cotswold gardens, and there is a group of four planted in a Cirencester shopping street.)

A fifteen-foot-high red brick wall divides the garden almost in half. Needless to say it has been put to very good use, with a wide mixed herbaceous and shrub border on one side, and climbers requiring less sun on the other. Guy Acloque says that the garden shuts down in September. Winter gardening is not for him. This being the case it is not surprising to see the south-facing border beneath the wall so wonderfully crammed with mostly summer-flowering plants. At one point last summer it was looking deliciously overflowing, bursting with colour and unfamiliar scents: 'a latter-day Helen Allingham', said Mr Acloque.

Roses play an important part in this border. Standards include 'Swany', a scrambler often used for ground cover or for draping itself on a low wall. Here it is grafted as a standard where its curtains of pure white, cupped double flowers tumble into the plants below. To all appearances 'Swany' is an 'old rose' but in fact it was bred in France little more than a decade ago, since the Acloques came here. 'Minnehaha', another prolific rose inclined to rambling, is also grown here as a standard, although *its* provenance is America, 1905. 'The Fairy' is a well-known and deservedly loved rose bred between the wars. Its small shell-pink flowers continue ceaselessly through the summer into autumn. 'Tuscany Superb', one of the best crimson roses, has broken its leash and begun to send up suckers between the paving cracks' – and I was delighted to see on a subsequent visit to Alderley that they had not been ripped up. A less familiar rose, 'Duc de Fitzjames', of unknown parentage, dates from Victorian times and occupies one end of the border near the house. At its feet grows the intriguing Moroccan mint which Guy Acloque brought back from a visit to the Atlas Mountains. This is the kind used for refreshing mint tea served everywhere in North Africa. Fennel, too, is another herb left to seed itself about in this border and its dainty filigree foliage makes it a welcome vagrant in this seemingly carefree style of planting. *Cotinus coggygria purpureus* picks up the tones of 'Tuscany Superb', and low-growing red double helianthemums weave through downy stachys and dark red sweet-williams, making a rich cardinal effect somewhat bolder in palette than many other borders of its type. Catmint and highlights of bright alchemilla break the straight edges of the paving between lawn and border, while inky delphiniums and cerulean campanulas spear the massed herbaceous geraniums whose foliage and pink flowers hide any trace of bare earth that might dare try to shew itself.

A gate in the wall at the right-hand side of this border leads through to the other half of the garden. Immediately in front, beckoning you through, is a short double row of pleached limes whose geometry

Palissade à l'italienne, Alderley Grange

makes jest of sense, and leads you to believe the shaded row is longer than it really is. Old pinks smelling of cloves seem to thrive without much sunshine – a good example of unexpected but spot-on plantsmanship. To one side on a neat square of grass is a weeping ash whose almost impenetrable crinoline allows access only to determined small birds.

In bright light at the end of the short lime tunnel there is a hedge of 'Sissinghurst Castle' or 'Rose des Maures', an old rose of uncertain origin 'rediscovered' at Sissinghurst in the 1940s. This hedge is clipped quite ruthlessly to keep it in some sort of decent shape but it goes on benevolently with its semi-double, maroon flowers.

We are now approaching nearer to Guy Acloque's heart, for here is one of those tight corners, with beds marked out in radiating hedges of low clipped box filled with herbs, sweet-smelling 'Ispahan' roses and wafting honeysuckles. Again, brick walls hold the warmth and help to contain the whiffs and fragrances emanating from the spicy tangle of aromatic plants. By now heartbeats should be racing and if you feel at all overcome with excitement there is a conveniently placed arbour shrouded in white wisteria where you can calm yourself. From this point, however, you will be facing a long path whose invitation to explore will be hard to refuse. It is hooped with yet more roses, honeysuckles and clematis and littered with pots of lemon verbena, sprawling nepeta, and clumps of curiously scented dictamnus releasing a volatile oil which can be ignited with a match to produce a magician's flash of flame without damage to the plant – *the* burning bush.

The next encounter is with a small pond full of water-lilies engulfed by white, yellow and peach-cloured foxgloves, and cistuses whose native home is the sun-baked hills around the Mediterranean. Two standard privets clipped as spheres, ceanothus and more roses form a backdrop where another seat is provided on an elevated level.

Tall standard-grown thorns, *Crataegus × lavallei* 'Carrierei' define a new area where begins what might be described as this garden's *coup de grâce* and the very valves of Mr Acloque's romantic heart. In a mist of yellow woad, henbane and purply aquilegias there is a spherical sundial which on sunny days tells the time for anyone still with a foot on the ground and not yet wholly seduced by the bombardment of unlikely colours, graceful shapes and piercing aromas. Clipped mophead privets with small leaves stand in a circle surrounding an urn with a tall box spiral. Contained within a very low hedge are white Florentine irises whose violet-scented roots, dried and powdered, are used as a fixative for the sweet oils in pot-pourri recipes.

Common herbs like sages and cotton-lavenders, lovage, dill, marjoram, chives, thymes, angelica and several mints all have their place, but unlike most herb gardens the commoners here have for their neighbours some of the most interesting and pungent of all known plants. Many may be tender or only half-hardy, grown outside in pots during the summer and carted off to spend the winter months somewhere dry and free of frost. Caraway thyme, the 'Herba Barona', is not on the list of special rarities but *Thymus mastichina* is seldom encountered in this country. It belongs to the Ronda Sierra in southern Spain where the Acloques spend much of their time when they are not in the Cotswolds. From Mexico and the south-eastern United States there is *Ptelea trifoliata* whose corymbs of greenish yellow flowers are among the most fragrant displayed by any tree. Their

Gazebo, Alderley Grange

perfume – supposedly an aphrodisiac – rivals the best honeysuckles. A plant whose special qualities have a similar aphrodisiacal effect, but on cats, is *Macromaria corsica*, a thyme-like herb with purple flowers in June. Guy Acloque also has a young sassafras tree which, when more mature, will provide him with aromatic bark. Another tree with essential oils in its bark is *Calycanthus floridus*, the Carolina allspice which has been known in cultivation here since 1726 – perhaps it was brought to this country on the same ship as the then newly-discovered catalpa.

Not all the unfamiliar herbs and aromatics in this garden are from distant parts. *Meum athamanticum* has been used for centuries in Scottish cooking but a glance at my only collection of recipes from Scotland ignores it completely. *Apium graveolens* is a native biennial wild celery whose flowers are adored by bees – hence its specific name; the full power of its characteristic smell is most noticeable on warm, damp days.

The unmistakable scent of lemon is not restricted to citrus bushes. There are lemon-scented geraniums, thymes and balms (*Melissa officinalis*) which may occur with plain green, variegated or golden leaves. And there is of course lemon verbena, which stands around this garden in pots wherever there is a space. These lippias are woody plants with a wayward habit but with the help of a cane they can easily be trained to a standard in one growing season. To me the smell of the crushed leaves is more like old-fashioned lemon-flavoured boiled sweets than the fresh tang of the fruit's real zest. More unusual to British nostrils is the lemon eucalyptus, *E. citriodora* from Australia, which will survive northern winters with the protection of a conservatory, although its vigorous growth will have to be cut back hard in restricted spaces. While turning out the pockets of a pair of summer trousers for a belated trip to the dry cleaners I found a dried lemon eucalyptus leaf whose pungency was as strong six months later as it had been on the June morning it was picked.

Guy Acloque grows a staggering number of aromatic plants. You will find cardamon in the greenhouse, balsam poplars, liquidambar and the incense rose, *Rosa primula*, in the garden; anise hyssop (another excellent bee plant) and Balm of Gilead are scattered around the working area in pots, together with prostantheras and a wonderful specimen of *Umbellularia californica*, the Californian bay, whose effective whiff was used in the nineteenth century to revive fainting ladies.

The fainting-lady phenomenon seems to have passed into history now, but luckily the plants that revived her, and the whole tribe of aromatics whose folklore and genuine 'official' use is so tangled and often dubious, live on in collections like this one on the edge of the Cotswolds. In their distant homelands many of them still yield their peculiar properties for tonics, vermouths, *tisanes*, medicines, and more than a handful of poisons. Fortunately Guy Acloque is well aware of the latter category and keeps them out of harm's way, but I think I would like rather more than his permission before I assigned some of the less familiar leaves to my stomach.

BIBLIOGRAPHY

Austin, David, *The Heritage of the Rose*, Antique Collectors' Club, 1988

Barkley, Sylvia Y., *Trees of Westonbirt School*, privately published

Beales, Peter, *Classic Roses*, Collins Harvill, 1985

Beales, Peter, *Twentieth-Century Roses*, Collins Harvill, 1988

Bean, W. J., *Trees & Shrubs Hardy in the British Isles*, Eighth edition (revised), John Murray, 1980

Betjeman, John, *Summoned By Bells*, John Murray, 1960

Brill, Edith, *Cotswold Crafts*, Batsford, 1977

Brown, Jane, *The English Garden in our Time*, Antique Collectors' Club, 1986

Brown, Jane, *The Art and Architecture of English Gardens*, Weidenfeld & Nicolson, 1989

Brown, Jane, 'Rodmarton Manor', *Hortus* 13 (Volume Four, number one, Spring 1990)

Clarke, Ethne, *Hidcote, The Making of a Garden*, Michael Joseph, 1989

Freeman, Margaret E., *Weston Birt*, privately published, 1977

Haslam, Richard, 'Newark Park, Gloucestershire', *Country Life* (3rd October, 1985)

Hatchett, David, *Country House Garden*, David & Charles, 1983

Hillier's Manual of Trees & Shrubs, Fifth edition, Hillier Nurseries (Winchester) Ltd., 1981

Hobhouse, Penelope, *Private Gardens of England*, Weidenfeld & Nicolson, 1986

Jellicoe, Geoffrey and Susan; Goode, Patrick and Lancaster, Michael, eds, *The Oxford Companion to Gardens*, Oxford University Press, 1986

Jewson, Norman, *By Chance I did Rove*, privately published, 1951

Johnson, Joan, *The Gloucestershire Gentry*, Alan Sutton Publishing, 1989

Kingsley, Nicholas, *The Country Houses of Gloucestershire: Volume One 1500–1660*, Nicholas Kingsley, 1989

Lees-Milne, Alvilde and Verey, Rosemary, eds, *The Englishwoman's Garden*, Chatto & Windus, 1980

Lees-Milne, Alvilde and Verey, Rosemary, eds., *The New English-woman's Garden*, Chatto & Windus, 1987

Lees-Milne, James, *Some Cotswold Country Houses*, Dovecote Press, 1987

Massingham, H. J., *Cotswold Country*, Batsford, 1937

Miles, Paul, 'Painswick Rococo Garden', *Hortus* 6 (Volume Two, number two, Summer, 1988)

Ottewill, David, *The Edwardian Garden*, Yale University Press, 1989

Parker, Jill, *The Purest of Pleasures*, Hodder & Stoughton, 1988

Rohde, Eleanour Sinclair, *The Story of the Garden*, The Medici Society, 1932 and 1989

Sherwood, Jennifer and Pevsner, Nikolaus, *The Buildings of England, Oxfordshire*, Penguin Books, 1974

Trehane, Piers, ed., *Index Hortensis* Volume One: Perennials, Quarterjack Publishing, 1989

Verey, David, *The Buildings of England, Gloucestershire: The Cotswolds*, Penguin Books, 1970

Verey, Rosemary, *The Scented Garden*, Michael Joseph, 1981

Verey, Rosemary, *Classic Garden Design*, Viking, 1984

Verey, Rosemary, *The Garden in Winter*, Windward/Frances Lincoln, 1988

Verey, Rosemary, *Good Planting*, Frances Lincoln, 1990

Verey, Rosemary, 'The making of an English Garden', *Hortus* 8, 9, 10 & 11 (Volume Two, number four, 1988, and Volume Three, numbers one, two and three, 1989)

THE PAINTINGS AND DRAWINGS

Artist's Note and Picture Dimensions

The pictures in this book are in either gouache and watercolour (some with applied paper), or ink. The paintings have been reduced to comply with page format; some of the drawings have been increased, others marginally reduced, some are same size.

Paintings and drawings exhibited at Upton Lodge Galleries, Tetbury, Gloucestershire, 27 May – 8 June 1991.

Gazebo, Alderley Grange 4″ × 2½″

Palissade à l'italienne, Alderley Grange 2½″ × 3½″

Woad, Alderley Grange 8″ × 11¾″

Beansticks, April Cottage 3″ × 4″

Cabbages and pansies, April Cottage 9¾″ × 9¾″

Hornbeam, Badminton House 3″ × 4¾″

The Laburnum Walk, Barnsley House 2¾″ × 4″

Late summer, Barnsley House 10″ × 11¾″

The marrow tunnel, Barnsley House 10¾″ × 8″

The Temple, Barnsley House 12¾″ × 9¾″
(Reproduced by kind permission of Dr and Mrs J. D. Sleath)

Pulsatilla vulgaris on the terrace, Beverston Castle 9¼″ × 12¾″

Staddle stones, Bourton House 7½″ × 11¾″

217

On the west side, Bourton House $2\frac{1}{2}'' \times 4\frac{3}{4}''$

The fountain in the hidden courtyard, Brewers Cottage $2\frac{1}{4}'' \times 2\frac{3}{4}''$

Tapestry, Broadwell House $10'' \times 11\frac{3}{4}''$

Topiary, Broadwell House $3\frac{1}{4}'' \times 5''$

The gravel walk, The Chipping Croft $8'' \times 11\frac{3}{4}''$

A West Highland terrier at The Chipping Croft $2\frac{1}{4}'' \times 2\frac{3}{4}''$

Betula jacquemontii avenue, Combend Manor $2\frac{3}{4}'' \times 4\frac{3}{4}''$

The view from the rock garden, Combend Manor $9\frac{1}{2}'' \times 8''$

On the East Terrace, Cornwell Manor $2\frac{1}{2}'' \times 3''$

A view from the formal pool, Cornwell Manor $13'' \times 10\frac{1}{2}''$

A view of the Water Garden, Cornwell Manor $2\frac{1}{4}'' \times 5\frac{1}{2}''$

In the terrace garden, Cotswold Farm $2\frac{3}{4}'' \times 3\frac{1}{4}''$

In the terrace garden in Autumn, Cotswold Farm $6'' \times 11\frac{3}{4}''$

The bust of a Caesar, Essex House $10\frac{1}{4}'' \times 8''$

The formal garden, Essex House $2\frac{1}{4}'' \times 5''$

Path to the pool, Ewen Manor $11'' \times 8''$

Steps to the terrace, Ewen Manor $3\frac{1}{4}'' \times 5''$

On approaching the garden at Greyhounds $2\frac{1}{2}'' \times 4\frac{3}{4}''$

Greyhounds at Greyhounds $2\frac{3}{4}'' \times 3\frac{1}{4}''$

The Fuchsia Garden in April, Hidcote Manor $8'' \times 11\frac{3}{4}''$

The Stilt Garden, Spring, Hidcote Manor $8'' \times 11\frac{3}{4}''$

Approaching sunset in the Kitchen Garden, Highgrove House $8'' \times 11\frac{1}{2}''$

In the Cottage Garden, Highgrove House $7\frac{1}{2}'' \times 9\frac{1}{2}''$

Doorway to the Park, Highgrove House $3\frac{1}{4}'' \times 4\frac{3}{4}''$

IMAGES OF COTSWOLD GARDENS

Sweet pea tunnel in the Kitchen Garden, Highgrove House $7\frac{3}{4}'' \times 12''$

The house, above a clamour of daisies, Hill House $3\frac{1}{4}'' \times 4\frac{1}{4}''$

Rose hoops, Hill House $8'' \times 11''$

Spring, Hodges Barn $8'' \times 10\frac{3}{4}''$

The house, from the rose garden, Hunts Court $13\frac{3}{4}'' \times 10''$

A mown path, Hunts Court $2'' \times 6''$

The garden, from across the drive, Kencot House $10'' \times 9''$

Summer-house, Kencot House $1\frac{1}{2}'' \times 5\frac{1}{2}''$

The garden front, Kiftsgate Court $7\frac{1}{4}'' \times 10''$

Mask, at the pool-side, Kiftsgate Court $2\frac{1}{2}'' \times 4''$

The Temple, Kiftsgate Court $8'' \times 11\frac{3}{4}''$

Whitebeam arch, Kiftsgate Court $3'' \times 4''$

The formal garden, The Little House $2\frac{3}{4}'' \times 4''$

The house from the lower garden, Little Tulsa $2\frac{1}{2}'' \times 2\frac{3}{4}''$

Poppies and delphiniums, Little Tulsa $8'' \times 8\frac{1}{4}''$

The dovecot overlooking the garden at Manor Farm $4'' \times 4''$

Garden path, Manor Farm $10'' \times 8\frac{3}{4}''$

Figure in the garden, Misarden Park $3'' \times 4\frac{1}{4}''$

The house above the terrace, Misarden Park $14\frac{1}{4}'' \times 10''$

A duck emerging from beneath *Pyrus salicifolia* 'Pendula', Newark Park $1'' \times 1\frac{1}{2}''$

The fort alongside the drive, Newark Park $2\frac{1}{2}'' \times 5\frac{1}{4}''$

A gateway, Newark Park $8'' \times 10\frac{1}{4}''$

The orangery, beside the lake, Newark Park $2\frac{1}{2}'' \times 4\frac{1}{2}''$

The garden beyond the walls, The Old Manor $9\frac{3}{4}'' \times 11\frac{1}{4}''$

Alliums in the Purple Border, The Old Post Office $10\frac{1}{4}'' \times 9''$

Father and child amongst the trees, The Old Post Office $3\frac{1}{2}'' \times 3\frac{1}{2}''$

In the small formal garden at The Old Rectory $3\frac{3}{4}'' \times 4''$

Verbascum in the Mixed Border at The Old Rectory $12'' \times 8\frac{1}{4}''$

Alcove in Painswick Rococo Garden $2\frac{1}{4}'' \times 4''$

Within the Red House, Painswick Rococo Garden $7\frac{3}{4}'' \times 11\frac{1}{2}''$
(Reproduced by kind permission of Mr and Mrs P. Elliott)

Sheets of *Anemone blanda*, Pinbury Park $12\frac{1}{2}'' \times 10''$

Topiary, Pinbury Park $3'' \times 3\frac{3}{4}''$

Pleached hornbeams, Poulton Manor $2\frac{1}{4}'' \times 3\frac{3}{4}''$

Rose 'The Alchemist', Poulton Manor $8'' \times 11\frac{3}{4}''$

Agapanthus and doorway, Rodmarton Manor $4'' \times 4''$

Summer-house, Rodmarton Manor $12'' \times 10\frac{1}{2}''$

The Topiary Garden, Rodmarton Manor $2'' \times 4''$

The Temple dedicated to Surya, Sezincote $2\frac{1}{2}'' \times 4\frac{3}{4}''$

In the cloisters, Sherborne Park $2\frac{1}{4}'' \times 4''$

The house, Stancombe Park $2\frac{1}{4}'' \times 5''$

Steps to the courtyard, Stancombe Park $11\frac{1}{2}'' \times 8\frac{1}{4}''$

A view across the lake, Stancombe Park $2\frac{3}{4}'' \times 3\frac{3}{4}''$

A first glimpse of the garden, Stowell Park $3\frac{1}{4}'' \times 4\frac{3}{4}''$

On the terrace, Stowell Park $7\frac{3}{4}'' \times 10\frac{1}{2}''$

Quatrefoil, Sudeley Castle $2'' \times 2\frac{1}{2}''$

The Queen's Garden, Sudeley Castle $3'' \times 6''$

On approaching the garden, Swinbrook House $2\frac{1}{2}'' \times 6''$

Lilies and campanula, Swinbrook House $10'' \times 9''$

IMAGES OF COTSWOLD GARDENS

Trullwell 3″ × 4″
(Reproduced by kind permission of Mr and Mrs M. Robinson)

Midsummer at Trullwell 10″ × 11¾″

The Herbaceous Walk, Upton Wold 9½″ × 9½″

The house, Upton Wold 3″ × 3½″

The Kitchen Garden, Upton Wold 10″ × 12½″

Irises, Snowshill Manor 10¾″ × 8¼″

Dad's Garden, Water Lane Farm 2¼″ × 6″

Stock beds, Water Lane Farm 8″ × 11¾″

The rose pergola, Waterton House 2¾″ × 5¼″

The house, from the formal garden, Westend House 1¾″ × 4¼″

A seat in a glade, Westend House 3¾″ × 3¾″

In the Italianate garden, Westonbirt School 8″ × 7½″

A cottage garden in Windrush 5¼″ × 7″

Summer flowers, Yew Tree Cottage 2¼″ × 2½″

INDEX

OVER THE HILLS FROM BROADWAY

Images of Cotswold Gardens

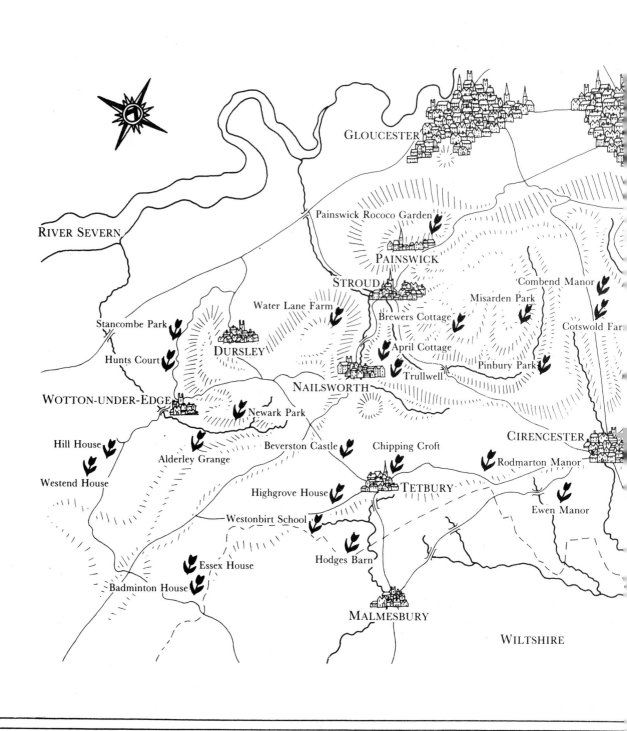

GLOUCESTER

RIVER SEVERN

Painswick Rococo Garden

PAINSWICK

STROUD

Combend Manor

Misarden Park

Water Lane Farm

Brewers Cottage

Cotswold Far

Stancombe Park

Hunts Court

DURSLEY

April Cottage

Pinbury Park

Trullwell

NAILSWORTH

WOTTON-UNDER-EDGE

Newark Park

CIRENCESTER

Hill House

Beverston Castle

Chipping Croft

Alderley Grange

Rodmarton Manor

Westend House

Highgrove House

TETBURY

Ewen Manor

Westonbirt School

Essex House

Hodges Barn

Badminton House

MALMESBURY

WILTSHIRE